HEALTH, HOPE, AND HEALING FOR ALL

TOWARD MORE EQUITABLE AND AFFORDABLE HEALTHCARE

EUGENE A. WOODS

FOREWORD BY MICHAEL WATKINS

Skyhorse Publishing

Skyhorse Publishing books may be purchased in bulk at special discounts for sales promotion, corporate gifts, fund-raising, or educational purposes. Special editions can also be created to specifications. For details, contact the Special Sales Department, Skyhorse Publishing, 307 West 36th Street, 11th Floor, New York, NY 10018 or info@skyhorsepublishing.com.

Skyhorse® and Skyhorse Publishing® are registered trademarks of Skyhorse Publishing, Inc.®, a Delaware corporation.

Visit our website at www.skyhorsepublishing.com.

10 9 8 7 6 5 4 3 2 1

Library of Congress Cataloging-in-Publication Data is available on file.

Cover design by Madelenn Tabor and David Ter-Avanesyan
Cover photo courtesy of Madelenn Tabor for Atrium Health

Print ISBN: 978-1-5107-7971-6
Ebook ISBN: 978-1-5107-7973-0

Printed in the United States of America

Contents

Foreword

When I met Gene in the spring of 2016, he was embarking on the journey that culminated in this book. He had been hired as the CEO of Carolinas HealthCare System and asked me to be his thought partner through his transition. I recall fondly the time we spent in his backyard, charting his first few months in the new role.

Fast-forward seven years, and he is leading one of the largest nonprofit healthcare systems in the United States. He is a nationally recognized healthcare executive, driver of innovation in the industry, and tireless advocate for health equity.

Early in his time leading the Carolinas organization, Gene worked with his board to develop the "Health, Hope, and Healing for All" mission statement, which is also the title of this book. I vividly remember him saying at the time, "It must be 'For All'" and thinking, "Wow, that's ambitious." Because Health, Hope, and Healing is a mission many healthcare systems could sign up for. But "For All" is a promise, and it was clear that he meant it.

Gene's journey took him and his organization into the fiery crucible of COVID-19. Inspired by his leadership, the renamed Atrium Health mobilized, innovated, persevered, and saved many lives. In the process, Gene got a deeper and broader view of how healthcare works (and doesn't) in America. He saw firsthand the inequities and inadequacies that are built into the system and resolved to take the lead in resolving them.

This book tells the story of Atrium Health and the COVID-19 crisis. It also puts forward eight powerful prescriptions that, if adopted, would change the U.S. healthcare system in fundamental and highly beneficial ways. Beyond much-needed improvements in overall efficiency and effectiveness, Gene's recommendations would address the profound challenges we face with health equity, not just for minorities but also for the working poor and people living in underserved rural communities.

On a personal note, Gene is one of the finest leaders I have had the privilege to work with as a coach and advisor. He is a consummate business strategist and a "cloud-to-ground" thinker. He's a visionary who foresaw the seismic shifts that have rocked the healthcare industry. He's a builder who has mobilized his team and organization to meet those challenges head-on.

He's also one of the finest people I know. Gene's devotion to realizing the promise of "For All" is real, deep, and enduring. Few business leaders have both the business savvy and the passionate commitment to doing what is right that he has. Like his music (and it's very unusual for a CEO also to be an accomplished songwriter and musician), Gene has true soul.

—Michael Watkins
July 2023

Author's Note
"I'm Hungry"

A distinguished-looking elderly man walked into the parking lot of Our Lady of Consolation Catholic Church in Charlotte's Double Oaks neighborhood. His clothes were rumpled from sleeping in them, and he badly needed a bath. He looked confused as he joined the line of folks wearing masks and waiting to be tested for COVID-19 at our Atrium Health Mobile Unit.

The man said he was looking for a soup kitchen, adding, "I'm hungry."

Double Oaks is located in what is known as "the crescent," a span of neighborhoods in Mecklenburg County characterized by a lack of economic development, educational resources, access to grocery stores, green space, and even sidewalks. The crescent arcs like an umbrella over top of "the wedge," where Charlotte's affluent have historically lived.

According to a report from the Robert Wood Johnson Foundation to the Commission to Build a Healthier America, adults living in poverty are more than five times as likely to report fair or poor health as those with incomes at least four times the Federal Poverty Line.[1] In Mecklenburg County overall, 22 percent of adults say they do not have a regular source of healthcare. Nearly as many admit they've not seen a doctor in years because they don't have enough money.

As president and CEO of one of the largest health systems in that nation and a person of color, I have devoted my career to helping to address the chasmic gaps that exist in health equity. In fact, that is the reason why one of our medical health vans was parked in one of the poorest neighborhoods in Charlotte outside Our Lady of Consolation on April 29, 2020.

The elderly man waited patiently in line until it was his turn. He said he was looking for food. He told us he had been homeless for the past three weeks. He had been living for a time with his sons in subsidized housing, but he could stay with them no longer. "If your name is not on the lease, they will kick out everyone from the house," he said. "And even though my boys wanted me to stay, I couldn't risk that for them . . . so I left."

He told us he had been sleeping in new construction sites and on the porches of vacant homes, leaving at first light before the workers arrived. And he was really hungry.

"One of our teammates immediately gave the man her boxed lunch," said Katy, our on-site social worker. "We found additional snacks in the RV for him, cleaned him up, and gave him a toothbrush and other supplies."

Nurse practitioner Stacy had freshly washed clothes in the trunk of her car that her husband had wanted to donate to Goodwill, so she made up a package of shirts, trousers, and shoes that fit him.

"He was so appreciative," said Stacy. "He kept saying, 'Thank you, thank you. God bless you.' He had tears in his eyes. And so did I."

Meanwhile, though the man was asymptomatic, our rapid test detected COVID-19. So Katy arranged transport for him to an isolation motel. North Carolina's Mecklenburg County had arranged to house homeless people there who tested positive but were not sick enough to be admitted to the hospital. There, community paramedics, part of our virtual hospital program, checked in on him daily. And Katy worked with the county to help the man find temporary housing.

This simple story of caring is not unique to Atrium Health. It was repeated countless times, in one form or another, by compassionate healthcare heroes throughout the nation during the most severe health emergency in our lifetimes. But for every heroic act performed, the pandemic has also exposed many deep, cataclysmic cracks in our healthcare system.

In fact, COVID-19 shone a harsh spotlight on the ugly reality of health disparities among communities of color. Black and Brown people have been far more likely to contract the coronavirus and be hospitalized, and they have been up to three times more likely to die than white Americans, according to the Centers for Disease Control and Prevention. We saw similar disparities in access to screening and vaccines—thus our efforts to use our community health mobile unit to work with grassroots organizations like Our Lady of Consolation to bring care directly to at-risk communities.

But, of course, racial disparities in healthcare existed long before the COVID-19 pandemic. Consider: A Black woman is three to four times more likely to die from pregnancy complications than a white woman. A Latino man is more likely to be diagnosed with colorectal cancer at later stages than a white man. A Native American teen is 50 percent more likely to commit suicide than those in the majority population. And, just recently, the *Journal of the American Medical Association* published research showing that 74,000 African Americans die annually because of pervasive health disparities.[2]

As the richest nation on earth, we can do better. Scratch that. We must do better. And we can. Our people are counting on us. And while the pandemic has tested our grit and resilience, we have demonstrated our ability to adapt, to be creative, and to act quickly and decisively together to overcome these types of challenges.

I wrote this book to document those changes and to illuminate a path forward based on what we've learned. I want to invite a dialogue for reforms on a national level and encourage other healthcare leaders to follow our lead or partner with us. We need to come together now. But our efforts must extend beyond the sobering realities of the pandemic.

What I hear from many well-intentioned people is that the problems feel so overwhelmingly big and complex that one doesn't even know where to begin or whether a real, measurable impact is even possible. My goal in this book is to challenge that fatalistic notion.

As I stated in my testimony to the U.S. Senate Health, Education, Labor, and Pensions Committee, on March 25, 2021:

> The COVID-19 pandemic has come at a great cost to the world. We should view this reality as an investment that allows us to emerge stronger. Through unity and collaboration,

government and industry are capable of great things. This has been, and still is, a core tenet of American exceptionalism. Much like when NASA was formed, and the power of partnership through technology landed Neil Armstrong on the moon, the possibilities of caring for and leading better lives—especially in the realm of health equity—are endless. Atrium Health's experiences this past year proves just that, whereby the value of bringing together the resources of government and industry have greatly supported the well-being of our population. So much so that, much like President Joe Biden's "Cancer Moonshot Initiative," we firmly believe a health equity moonshot is also not out of reach.

What our Atrium teammates did that day for an elderly homeless man illustrates the true heart of this nation's citizens. And the task before us is to systemize that type of care and intervention on a macro level in order to achieve our vision of helping people reach their highest potential for health. And that also requires that we address the fundamental determinants of health before people end up in a hospital—a safe home, a job, access to healthy, affordable food, and green spaces for exercise and recreation. And given the trauma and lessons of the pandemic, Dr. Martin Luther King's words have never rung so true: "We are now faced with the fact that tomorrow is today. We are confronted with the fierce urgency of now. In this unfolding conundrum of life and history, there is such a thing as being too late."[3]

A Call for Collaboration

I wrote this book as a fierce call to action now, based on lessons I've learned from leading health systems in this nation over the past thirty years—from rural to urban, regional to national, and government to nonprofit health systems.

Here is the thing . . . nearly twenty years ago, the Institute of Medicine (now the National Academy of Medicine) published a seminal work called *Unequal Treatment: Confronting Racial and Ethnic Disparities in Healthcare*. Commissioned by Congress, the study conducted by a panel of fifteen experts explored how people of color experience the healthcare environment and documented evidence of disparities in treatment that arise out of those clinical encounters. The 764-page report was unequivocal in finding that "Racial and ethnic minorities experience a lower quality of health services and are less likely to receive even routine medical procedures than are white Americans."[4] Two decades later, sadly, the gaps remain.

But I'm undaunted. Today we have an incredible opportunity to work together to revolutionize healthcare for the good of the country and our citizens.

Healthcare systems, though, cannot tackle this ambitious task list alone. We need to do it with government officials and business leaders working together in close partnership with community organizers and religious and civic organizations. And we need to do it now, amid our struggle to emerge from the grip of the pandemic and heal a deeply divided nation. I hold onto the firm conviction that with courage, compassion, and civility we can come together to improve health, elevate hope, and advance healing—for all.

—Eugene A. Woods
July 15, 2023

CHAPTER 1

"This Is for Real"

March 11, 2020

Twenty-one passengers on a cruise ship off the California coast test positive for SARS-CoV2. Five days later, the World Health Organization declares the novel coronavirus a global pandemic. Four days after the WHO announcement, COVID-19 claims its first lives in New York City.

It was coming our way.

We didn't know how long it would be until the virus would show up in hospitals in North Carolina, but, no doubt, it would be soon.

I had tremendous confidence in the talented leadership team at Atrium Health, as well as in our frontline doctors, nurses, and support staff—but having been through several major hurricanes, I knew one thing for sure: No matter what the meteorologist predicts, you can really never know the severity of a hurricane until it reaches your doorstep. And I recalled a military saying I once heard: no plan remains intact upon first contact with the enemy.

In early February, emergency department doctor David Callaway, MD, Atrium Health's chief of crisis operations, was flying back to Charlotte from Geneva, Switzerland, where he had attended a World Health Organization meeting of international disaster response leaders. He had a knot in his stomach, and it wasn't from the airline food. A former navy combat physician, Dr. Callaway is chief medical officer for

Team Rubicon, an organization of U.S. military veterans that deploys WHO-backed emergency medical units to natural disasters and humanitarian crises around the world. Dr. Callaway had been invited to the WHO meeting to help craft new standards of medical care in conflict zones. But the underlying buzz at the conference was the outbreak in Wuhan. The U.S. State Department had just evacuated staff from China.

Wedged into the middle seat of a Boeing 757 for the thirteen-hour flight home, Dr. Callaway couldn't shake his uneasy feeling.

"I didn't get it at first," he told me a few days later. "At the conference, everybody was freaking out about Wuhan, but I thought, 'There's just one paper out of China about this novel coronavirus, and it described it as being like the flu, with a one and a half percent mortality.' I'm like, 'Is this really going to be *that* big of a deal?'"

Dr. Callaway had been chatting at the meeting with a team of Australian doctors, the first ones to bring up the notion that the virus had originated in a biolab.

"The Aussies told me that they felt this was going to be *very* big and very bad," he said.

What worried Dr. Callaway most, however, was the lack of information coming from reliable scientific sources. Everyone seemed to be guessing at what we were dealing with. Dr. Callaway had served as a field physician with the 3rd Marines for three years in Iraq, El Salvador, and Burma. He was used to working with limited and ever-changing data. But this looming crisis seemed different to him somehow, simply because of its potential scale.

Back in Charlotte, Dr. Callaway quickly called meetings with other physicians and colleagues in what was then a forty-four-hospital system, to share what he had learned and to begin preparing for the unknown.

* * *

Days later, on a brisk afternoon in Charlotte, with a cloudless sky and bright sunshine streaming through my office window, I looked at the beautiful skyline and reflected on how proud I was of the work the team was doing on so many fronts. In recent years, we had changed our name from Carolinas HealthCare System to Atrium Health, to better reflect our growth trajectory and aspirations to grow beyond North Carolina and build a national system. (Not long before the publication of this book, we changed again, combining with Advocate Aurora Health.)

Our new mission statement, "To improve health, elevate hope, and advance healing—for all," had taken firm root in our culture. And we were delivering on that promise.

Our community investment effort had never been more ambitious. We partnered with community organizations to create food pantries in physicians' offices, to prescribe fresh and nutritious foods to patients in need. We trained local barbers and hairstylists and other community members—12,000 in all—to recognize signs of mental illness and guide clients to behavioral health services. And we had committed $10 million to affordable housing, because we know that a safe place to live, healthy foods, and access to quality healthcare are critical to one's overall health.

We had also recently celebrated a milestone at Atrium Health: our eightieth birthday since first opening doors as Charlotte Memorial Hospital in 1940. The founders could not have possibly imagined that from that single hospital would arise a system of over forty hospitals and nearly 1,000 care sites. And now we were embarking on the most ambitious building project in our history. With a $2 billion investment in our facilities, we would modernize the system and infuse it with the latest technology and designs, to create healing environments that would serve communities for decades to come. In addition, in the past three years, we had added three tremendous new partners. We brought Navicent Health in Macon, Georgia, into our system, as well as Georgia's Floyd Health, and were preparing to bring Wake Forest Baptist Health with its Wake Forest University School of Medicine into the family. The latter would include building a new medical school campus in Charlotte, one of the largest cities in the nation without one.

And yet, despite all of the positive momentum, I had a deep feeling of unease after receiving a call from Jim Hunter, MD, our senior vice president and chief medical officer. "Gene, we need to brief you on this virus ASAP," he said. Dr. Hunter also headed up our Incident Command Emergency Response, and Dr. Callaway reported to him in that structure. Hunter had been with the system for a couple decades and always had a steady-at-the-wheel, never-get-rattled demeanor about him. But I detected something in his voice I hadn't heard before. Whatever it was we were about to face, it felt menacing.

I placed a call to Dena Diorio, the Mecklenburg County manager. "Hey, Dena, I am hearing on the ground that this thing could be really bad," I said. "I'm thinking we should start mobilizing all the community agencies and begin preparing for worst-case contingency scenarios."

On March 10, six days before the WHO pandemic announcement, I was watching the president's nightly press conference for updates from doctors Birx and Fauci. President Trump took the podium: "We're prepared and we're doing a great job with it," he said. "And it will go away. Just stay calm. It will go away."

In my brain I was trying to reconcile that statement with scenes from New York City I'd seen on the news and what I was increasingly hearing from my CEO colleagues there: ED doctors and nurses sitting exhausted on the floors of hallways crowded with patients; ICU nurses shedding their scrubs in their garages and sleeping on basement couches, for fear of infecting their families; shortages of personal protective equipment. (The nation quickly learned new hospital jargon—"PPE.")

The next day, March 11, I walked into the boardroom of our corporate headquarters for the briefing that Dr. Hunter had called. Seated at the table were Atrium Health's medical director for infection prevention, Katie Passaretti, MD; Shelley Kester, RN, head of infection prevention; Pam Beckwick, RN, who ran quality and patient safety; and Dr. Hunter.

Until that day, I'd only had a few interactions with Dr. Passaretti, a Johns Hopkins–trained physician with a stellar reputation throughout the system, regarded as much for her smarts as her personable approach. She has a way of instantly creating trust and credibility, as well as the ability to explain the dizzying science of infectious disease in terms that anyone, *even a CEO*, could understand.

After explaining what we knew and mostly what we didn't know about this novel virus, she didn't mince words. "This could be," she said, "one of the most significant challenges we have ever faced, and we will need to take immediate action on everything from protective equipment, to whether we let people travel, to how many people could be in a room." We all glanced at each other. She went on: "Perhaps most importantly, our people are frightened; they're seeing what's happening in New York and wondering, 'Do we need full body protection? Will we have patients in the hallways, too? What if we bring the virus home to our families?' So, we are going to have to launch an aggressive communication strategy as well."

Dr. Passaretti was somber but poised. I knew she had helped lead through big infectious disease challenges before. In 2009, the system battled the H1N1 virus, which primarily affected children, young people, and middle-aged adults, and we were able to save many lives. So, I had confidence in our battle-tested team. But this was sounding a heck of a lot more severe than H1N1. And I was also already thinking that, in addition to keeping people safe, we would be battling fear itself.

"This looks like something none of us have ever faced, Gene," Dr. Hunter said. "I recommend immediately implementing our Incident Command Emergency Response structure"—and after a pause, he added, "across the entire enterprise. It'll be all hands on deck, around the clock."

ICER is an emergency protocol for managing disasters. It was first developed in the 1970s, following a series of catastrophic fires in California. It's designed to streamline decision-making in times of crisis, facilitate interdepartmental interfaces by bringing together all key stakeholders and decision-makers, and escalate response according to the severity of the crises. I approved, knowing it would immediately shift organizational priorities, work flows, and focus.

We then talked about the nuts and bolts of preparing for the first cases, which we believed we'd start seeing in a matter of days. The team had already begun thinking through the next chess moves. One of the first tasks would be voluntarily canceling non-emergent surgeries, to create capacity, including converting operating rooms into intensive-care units, as needed. Plans were also launched to explore building a tent hospital for overflow patients. We talked through other critical decisions that would need to be made over the next week, including staffing.

That evening, I called my former wife, Ramona, who was living in Reading, Pennsylvania. "This doesn't look good," I said. "We should tell the boys and your mother to avoid crowds."

Then I phoned my mother and sister in Warminster, Pennsylvania. "Mamá, tienes que tener cuidado (*Mom, you have to be careful*)," I said in Spanish, her first language. "The virus is tough on older folk. Wash your hands a lot. I'm going to send you up some masks. Make sure you wear them whenever you go out."

I also prepared a message to our Atrium Health teammates, to let them know that I, together with the entire senior team, had their backs, that we were in this together, and that I felt and heard the deep concerns they had for their families, friends, neighbors, and each other.

Over the next few days, I started making rounds in the hospitals, speaking to frontline staff, hearing their concerns directly, trying in whatever way I could to project a sense of calm and that we got this. I conveyed the same message in my video address to teammates, although internally the pit in my stomach was becoming a constant companion. We also quickly circulated staff surveys to get a temperature check. We knew people were scared, so we asked: "What are you worried about? What do you need? What are your concerns?"

If there's one thing I've learned about leading in my thirty years of hospital work, it's that there is tremendous power in just listening and then acting on what you hear, whenever you can, as that builds trust in leadership.

The survey responses were consistent: "I'm worried about bringing this home to my family." So, we immediately planned with local hotels to have our staff quarantine there after shifts if they had concerns. "Who will take care of my kids when I am at work?" That concern led us to work with the local YMCA on COVID-19-safe daycare protocols, and we expanded our benefits by waiving the copay on center-based and in-home childcare, offering up to $100 a day in subsidy for people who wanted to hire their own childcare providers. And lastly: "I am exhausted when I come home and barely have the strength to make food." The entire Charlotte community seemed to respond with food drives for our teams . . . the pizza kept coming and coming.

After reviewing this feedback at one of my CEO council meetings, I said, "Despite the turbulence, we will need to continue to navigate through. Let's remember to keep the main thing in mind: protect our patients, protect our teammates, protect our community." It was a simple way to bring clarity to our key mission, and it ended up being a powerful unifying message. Those three goals got people moving in the right direction. It filled the vacuum of uncertainty, so we wouldn't get distracted by the chaos.

And we knew there would be chaos. We saw it play out through our TVs and laptop screens in our living rooms every night. Most disturbing were the refrigerated semitrailers parked on New York City streets as makeshift morgues.

But I also shared that my hope for us as a team was that, many years from now, when we looked back on these times, we could tell our grandchildren that when our community needed us most, the best of who we were showed up. I did everything I could to keep people positive. As a high school athlete, I knew the power of an upbeat halftime pep talk from the head coach, though I was well aware we were likely still very much in the first quarter of this game.

The main thing keeping us up at night was getting our hands on real-time useful data. And that was really hard to come by. We absorbed everything the CDC was putting out there, but this was new to them, too, and it felt like they were playing catch-up.

I called Derek Raghavan, MD, PhD, president of our Levine Cancer Institute at Atrium Health, because I recalled that he had recruited physicians on his team with connections to China. Sure enough, two doctors on his staff had been born in mainland China, one he had recruited from MD Anderson Cancer Center and another from the Cleveland Clinic. Dr. Raghavan said one of the doctors actually went to medical school in Wuhan. I asked if they could arrange a call directly with their friends and colleagues in Wuhan, to find out what were they doing that was working, what wasn't, and anything else they could tell us about the spread of the virus.

Another Levine oncologist, Jubilee Brown, MD, who was president of an international gynecologic laparoscopy society, started talking with her members, which led to the creation of a full symposium on COVID-19 and cancer, involving doctors from France, Germany, Spain, the UK, and other countries. Yet another Levine colleague had connections with the Ministry of Health in Taiwan.

"We have data directly from the field, from people internationally, with frontline experience with the virus," Dr. Raghavan told me. "My conclusion is we'll have to do pretty draconian stuff: mask everyone, stop visitors, and lock down the cancer center immediately."

So, we began to implement actions I could never have contemplated in my thirty years of hospital work, starting with shutting down everything that wasn't emergent or critical, including elective surgeries, in order to open beds wherever we could, even in hallways if necessary. It felt like we were a big MASH (mobile army surgical hospital) unit, just behind the front lines, preparing for a wave of casualties to arrive.

Maureen Swick, PhD, who was our senior vice president and system nurse executive, told me she felt fortunate that we had a little bit of time to learn from the hardest-hit areas before the virus reached North Carolina. "We were given a very small gift of time to plan," she said. "We will use that time wisely."

Swick, who represented more than 15,000 nurses throughout the Atrium Health system, redeployed thousands of nurses to emergency departments and critical care units from ambulatory sites that had been closed due to COVID-19. A few weeks' warning gave her the window to put together learning modules, to train those nurses who hadn't been in acute care settings, so they could be an extra pair of hands in the hospital under the direction of a critical care registered nurse.

Overnight, we also converted our back-office support teams, over 10,000 employees, to work at their home offices. That included everyone who had secure computer stations. Nonhospital clinical teammates began working remotely to support frontline staff and limit exposure and spread of the virus.

By June 2020, U.S. healthcare lost more than 1.4 million jobs, and many hospitals had to lay off workers to remain financially stable. We decided neither to furlough nor lay anyone off. It was part of our core commitment to have teammates' backs on something that wasn't anyone's fault. And the last thing we wanted was to have people worried about not just their lives, but their incomes.

Fortunately, we had the balance sheet strength to keep paying wages and benefits. But something else played into the decision not to furlough. I knew we already had a shortage of staff coming into the pandemic, and we'd certainly need people to get us out. If you deconstruct your labor force and then try to rehire, you'll find yourself in a very tenuous situation. So, instead, we focused on retaining our teammates.

Notwithstanding, our operating finances were taking a severe hit. By the end of 2020, we had lost $300 million. Some of that was mitigated by CARES Act funding to keep our cash flow going so we could pay for PPE, ventilators, and other needed supplies. But I told my team, "Listen, we will worry about our finances later. For now, we stay focused on patients, teammates, and community."

Regarding teammates, we beefed up plans to support staff facing hardships by adding to our Caregiver Heroes Teammate Emergency Care Fund. I committed $1 million as seed money into the fund, which was matched by Atrium Health's senior team. That $2 million led to other matching philanthropic funds. Ultimately, it led to a $5 million fund that was made available to teammates who were experiencing hardships beyond their control.

Dr. Hunter was giving me several updates each day on our situation throughout the enterprise. He also crafted a newsletter called the *Daily Brief* that was sent to all physicians with assessments on our current capabilities, supplies, and a bed census, as well as the latest news on the spread of the virus nationally and intel on treatments. We included how many days' supply we had on hand for gloves, sanitizer, gowns, etc. There were many times when supplies were running in the red, with less than a week of availability. I sometimes felt like the chief supply officer, versus the chief executive officer, because I was calling everyone I knew for PPE, ventilators, and more.

A call to my friend Darius Adamczyk, the CEO of Honeywell, scored a week's supply of masks. It was definitely an all-hands-on-deck effort, with no job too big or small for anyone.

The War Room

I first came to know our emergency department leader, Dr. David Callaway, through my former chief of staff, Debra Plousha Moore, who was one of his mentors. Debra described Dr. Callaway as "the grenade I throw into the room when I want to shake things up." He's the kind of person you want leading crisis operations. He gets things done and asks for forgiveness later.

A few weeks into the pandemic, I wanted to see how things were going in the emergency department, so I met Dr. Callaway outside the ED entrance of our flagship Atrium Health Carolinas Medical Center in downtown Charlotte. He was wearing a baseball cap backward with the words *Audentis fortuna iuvat* embroidered on the back.

"What's that on your hat?" I asked.

He pronounced it in Latin. "It means 'fortune favors the bold.' I think it's Virgil. Some army friends who work in hostage rescue gave it to me."

"Love that," I said. "Great message for what we are dealing with."

Dr. Callaway led me into a large triage tent in the parking lot, staffed by active-duty military personnel and Team Rubicon members.

"We're screening patients here before they get to the physical structure," he explained. "If they think they've got COVID-19, or they're scared, or if they're here for some other health problem, they get screened in the tent, sometimes without even getting out of their car, before going home or going inside."

"Cool. Who authorized this so quickly?" I asked.

"Um, we did."

"Fortune favors the bold," I laughed.

When you're a hospital system as large and complex as ours, it takes some time to turn the ship. That's why we deploy an incident command system (ICS), to respond quickly and scale it to fit the magnitude of the emergency. COVID-19 taught us that even proven emergency management planning like ICS needs to be flexible. But we also took a page out of General Stanley McChrystal's "team of teams" approach. As leader of the Joint Special Operations Task Force fighting al-Qaeda in Iraq, Gen. McChrystal quickly concluded that conventional warfare tactics weren't working. The operation had to become more agile and make faster decisions. So, he transformed the massive military organization in Iraq into a team of teams—smaller groups that were given the freedom to experiment, respond more quickly, and share what they learned more freely. It gave frontline leaders in the field the authority to make decisions on the spot, without slogging through the normal chain of command based on what they knew was the commander's intent. In this case, again, our mission was to protect our people, patients, and community.

And that kind of team-of-teams approach to streamline decision-making was essential for departments like our emergency department, which was like a war zone, with staff improvising for each new challenge they faced.

Dr. Callaway and his colleagues commandeered a large conference room in the medical center and rearranged the tables in a large square so the team could socially distance eight feet apart. They set up computers, dry-erase boards, and two large video monitors, to track national news and the emerging data from Johns Hopkins. They called it the War Room.

Dr. Callaway took me inside. On the walls were American flags and motivational quotes from Teddy Roosevelt, Winston Churchill, and other leaders.

"You must never be fearful of what you are doing when it is right," read a Rosa Parks poster.

A large sheet of paper taped to a wall listed "8 Rules of the War Room." Number 3, "Be Kind." Number 6, "Think 5 Steps Ahead." But Number 5 threw me. It read, "Change Your Socks." Dr. Callaway explained that it's a military expression, meaning: make sure team members take care of themselves, stop for rest breaks, and never forget to eat. They were working sixteen-hour shifts. These were motivated, selfless professionals; they needed to be reminded that they must take care of themselves to be able to care for others.

From the War Room, the team coordinated with groups across the Atrium Health system, monitoring the number of intensive-care beds in case of a surge in coronavirus patients. When they realized they had only four days' worth of N95 masks, they worked the phones, calling vendors in search of supplies. Dr. Callaway told me that one ED doctor had a contact at 3M with a supply of "elastomeric respirators" with electrostatically charged particulate filters that were reusable. He could get fifty at $4.79 apiece.

"Buy them now before they disappear," Dr. Callaway told the doctor. "The hospital will reimburse you." So, three ED doctors and a paramedic put the order on their personal credit cards.

Atrium Health staff reordered the reusable masks numerous times, saving 15,000 N95s over the course of 2020.

A Voice of Calm amid Chaos

We often hear in the news about the psychological stress of frontline clinical staff tirelessly battling the pandemic. It is real. It is not often that you also hear about the heavy emotional burden borne by committed management teams who needed to make critical decisions with a dearth of reliable data and guidance that was often conflicting—while knowing thousands of lives hung in the balance. Staff were scared. People were seeing more death than they had in their whole professional careers. And on top of all that, we are a large health system, full of scientists and doctors who are trained to have the right answers. Recommendations were coming to Dr. Passaretti from all corners.

And the stress she felt during the early days of the pandemic was monumental.

I knew she was feeling the weight of the barrage of differing views—and so I called her late one evening.

"How are you doing?" I said.

"Well, I could be much better. I am doing everything I can to navigate through this, but I can't lie, it is wearing on me. Plus I get that everyone has an opinion on how to manage through this, but I need space to process and need to know that you have confidence in me to do so."

"I have one hundred percent confidence," I replied. "I completely have your back."

I knew that our decision structure couldn't fracture amid interprofessional tensions, which were understandable given the circumstances. And I needed to provide a buffer for Dr. Passaretti. After all, she was also the face of our pandemic response in the press and on TV. As our pandemic "emcee," she had the ideal style. She is a professional, a scientist who knows what she's talking about, and she gives people a feeling of comfort in uncertain times. She was exactly who we needed to instill confidence and calm.

So, I called our chief physician executive, Scott Rissmiller, MD, a can-do leader you would want in any foxhole with you. He set up weekly calls with all the key physician leaders to provide a clearinghouse for the best ideas and to funnel and filter clinical information while maintaining an organized systemwide approach. All these dynamics of organizational behavior are the little nuances of the pandemic that few people have visibility into, but they speak to the complexity of a crisis like this when the stakes are so high for every single decision made.

Two years after the start of the pandemic, I had a chance to chat with Dr. Hunter before he retired and reflect on what we had been through. "It's easy for people to forget how scared everyone was at the beginning," he said, "how little we knew. We didn't have vaccines. We didn't have medications. We didn't know how it spread. We thought we might end up like Italy, with people literally dying in the halls. Could that be us?"

It was a period of intense fear. And everyone felt it. But how we made it through was not a miracle. We improvised, stayed agile, called audibles, pulled together tightly as a team, checked in on one another, and always—always—started with what is the right thing to do if it were our loved ones or friends we were caring for. Many times, it was.

Hospital at Home

As we watched the rapid spread of COVID-19, as it stretched hospital capacity across the country to the brink, we ran numerous scenarios on how to accommodate the overflow we knew was coming, which would stretch every available space we had and then some.

One thing was clear: technology would have to play a key role. Working with Microsoft, we developed online algorithms based on the latest CDC guidance and sent them to more than one million patients with information about COVID-19, including how to get care from home. We instructed all ambulatory patients with nonemergency COVID-19 symptoms to use virtual or e-visits as their first method of care.

Meanwhile, Dr. Rissmiller assembled a multidisciplinary team of clinicians and administrators to address the looming capacity crisis and sent me a proposal that had been on the drawing board for some time before the pandemic on how to convert a patient's own bedroom into a hospital room. It was an idea whose time had come. I approved the rapid deployment of a pilot, and in just ten days the team launched a two-unit virtual hospital. We have cared for thousands of patients in their own homes since the start of the pandemic, ensuring hospital beds are available for the sickest patients.

We called it "hospital at home." Here's how it worked: Patients who didn't require the level of care they'd get in, say, an intensive-care unit received a COVID-19 home monitoring kit, which included a blood pressure monitor, pulse oximeter, and thermometer, so our care team could remotely monitor their vital signs twenty-four hours a day. We provided two levels of care—observation care and acute care. The VACU, or virtual acute care unit, is for patients who have more serious symptoms that would normally require admittance to the hospital. We set those patients up with a hospital bed, medical equipment, and videoconferencing tools within twenty-four hours. Then we followed up with oxygen assistance and other medical treatments, if needed, with daily virtual physician rounds, twice-daily nursing assessments, and vital sign monitoring.

We started this program in the very beginning of the pandemic. Between the end of March and early that May, Atrium Health Hospital at Home had treated 1,477 patients, which made up 64 percent of all our COVID-19 patients during that period. And of the 1,293 patients in virtual observation units, only 3 percent required inpatient hospitalization. Ultimately, we became the largest provider of hospital at home care in the entire country.

But here's the part that really made me think this was a strategy that would be useful beyond the pandemic: Our quality outcomes with patients in the Hospital at Home program appeared to be similar to those with inpatient hospital stays. Initially, though, the government didn't know how to reimburse hospitals for these services. Alex Azar, who was the U.S. Secretary of Health and Human Services (HHS), heard about the innovative practices we were deploying and did his very first site visit during the COVID-19 pandemic to our health system to learn more. We gathered about twenty-five of our leaders in an oversized conference room, all masked up and each separated by six feet, and walked him through all the creative initiatives we had launched. We shared with him how we were preparing our Med-1 Mobile Hospital as a state-of-the-art emergency room to travel to our hardest-hit areas, and we described to him our hospital at home program.

Secretary Azar and I connected over the number of things we had in common. He is from Pennsylvania, as I am, and he is also a graduate of Yale, where my youngest son was then studying, albeit remotely. He got it immediately, when we shared that the hospital at home program was working, but that we needed to think through a reimbursement pathway, because there was no way to bill for the care.

"Let's connect our people next week and work on that, because it will help other systems as well," he said.

Within weeks, and with our input, HHS had developed a waiver program that provided hospitals a diagnosis-related group payment for the duration of the public health emergency period. Ultimately, we published numerous reports, including in *Annals of Internal Medicine*, one of the most influential specialty medical journals in the world. The study, "Factors Associated with Rising Risk for Care Escalation Among Patients with COVID-19 Receiving Home-Based Hospital Care," was published May 10, 2021[1], and was the first to detail the findings that presented oxygen saturation and suggested that other chronic illnesses should be considered appropriate for hospital-level care at home.

The Million Mask Initiative

From day one, we knew that wearing masks was one of the best ways to reduce risk of disease transmission. But it was becoming very political: the debate was being framed as public safety versus personal freedom. Further complicating the issue, by late May and into June, masks were in very short supply.

On the night of June 24, 2020, North Carolina Governor Roy Cooper contacted me, to see if I would join him in two days when he announced his executive order mandating the use of face masks in public. It was clear that a mask mandate would be controversial in a purple state like North Carolina, so Cooper wanted our support as the state's largest health system. As the chair of the Federal Reserve Bank of Richmond during this time, I also knew how inextricably connected successfully battling COVID-19 was to the economic health of the country. The faster we could get the pandemic under control, the faster business could open up again. So, I decided to call my business colleagues for support and to ask them to donate some of the masks they might have in inventory.

My first call was to Brian Moynihan, CEO of Bank of America. Brian said he was all in. Then I called the CEO of Lowe's Home Improvement, Marvin Ellison. He was in, too. Within forty-eight hours—after conversations with Ric Elias, the CEO of Red Ventures, David Tepper, owner of the Carolina Panthers, Darius Adamczyk, CEO of Honeywell, and others—I walked onto the stage with the governor and announced we had a commitment of one million masks from the business community, with a commitment to distribute them to the most vulnerable populations. That was the beginning of a public-private partnership that would be foundational to how we managed the pandemic.

I have come to realize that whenever you're facing complex societal problems and decisions like this, you've got to have that trifecta of business leaders, health professionals, and government officials in the game. And this mask initiative, we hoped, could become a national example of how that trifecta can work together to make a significant positive impact on the community while spurring the local economy.

The Million Mask Initiative gelled quickly. After a call to Mecklenburg County Public Health Director Gibbie Harris, she agreed to join our task force. Our goal was to get masks on the faces of everyone in the region and to go where people needed them . . . like church parking lots, construction sites, and retail stores.

Supply of masks was one challenge. Getting people to wear them was another. We had to make mask-wearing acceptable and also cool. So, on social media, we partnered with athletes and community leaders to reach people on their terms. It was an all-hands-on-deck initiative.

By September 2020, as we were closing in on two million masks distributed in our communities, total COVID-19 cases had dropped 21 percent, and the positivity rate had dropped from 7.7 percent to 6.9 percent. Mecklenburg County, the primary target of the Million Mask Initiative, saw total daily positive rates drop by more than 60 percent and positivity rates drop by over 50 percent.

It was exciting to see the statistical data come in and be able to correlate it with the mask initiative. We noted that the more masks that were distributed, the fewer positive cases were being reported.

We didn't let up. By June the following year, the initiative had tripled its original goal, providing three million masks to our faith communities, small businesses, daycare centers, local universities, gyms, breweries, and neighborhood associations.

Silver Linings and New Life

Even though Atrium Health shut down noncritical functions throughout our system, during the first months of the pandemic, we still needed to treat the normal emergencies of hospital life—burst appendixes, heart attacks, car accidents, babies who needed to be ushered into the world, and those aberrant situations like heart transplants.

On March 13, the day President Trump declared COVID-19 a national emergency, a South Carolina pastor named Steven Evans was waiting in a hospital bed at Atrium Health Sanger Heart & Vascular Institute with a temporary ventricular assist device supplying his body with blood and oxygen.

Evans had heart failure. He needed a transplant, and his time was running out.

Doctors turned down available hearts twice before they found the right one. Evans had been waiting for two weeks. Fortunately, a new high-tech version of that life-giving heart pump acted as a critical bridge to the transplant, keeping his energy up while he waited. He calculated how many laps around the ICU it would take to walk a mile: sixteen. He started walking. By the time a heart had been found, he was doing twenty laps a day.

On March 20, during the chaos of COVID-19 hospitalizations, Evans received his new heart. It was the nineteenth heart transplant Sanger surgeons had performed during the first four months of 2020. Eight days later, Steven Evans went home to his wife and four daughters—and a new life.

I remember thinking to myself, during those early days of the pandemic, "We're dealing with a category five hurricane." But, wow, I was so impressed with and grateful for how the team was battling the storm—and though they were exhausted, they had a "never quit" attitude about them. I picked up the copy of *The Art of War* that I keep on my desk and read, "If you know the enemy and know yourself, you need not fear the result of a hundred battles."

We knew ourselves and were starting to know the enemy. I felt we would make it through, though I had no idea how many battles there were still to fight.

CHAPTER 2

Vaccines and New Hope

When the Moderna, Pfizer, and Johnson & Johnson vaccines received emergency-use authorization from the FDA, it felt like finally there was a way out of these hellish times. One of the best days in my career was being there in person to see the first of our frontline teammates be vaccinated. Our teammates were people from all walks of life, who put themselves in harm's way, every single day, to save others. Now they wouldn't have to risk their own lives to do so. I put the very first empty vial of the vaccine in my pocket as a keepsake, so I would never forget the moment.

While watching those first vaccinations with joy, I recalled being interviewed by Margaret Brennan on *Face the Nation*, back on July 26, 2020[1], six months earlier. The segment foretold the challenges we would soon experience.

> **MARGARET BRENNAN:** Are you going to ask in your conversations with Congress for your healthcare workers to be at the front of the line for a vaccine? And what do you see happening with distribution of it?
> **WOODS:** Yes, we have asked that healthcare workers throughout the country, especially in the hot spot areas, be at the front of the line together with essential workers, including teachers and so forth. So, we've already made that request. The challenge, and I shared this with the Senate committee,

is that, you know, even when we have a flu season, 40 percent of Americans say they're not going to get vaccinated. And so what you heard in my testimony was that I do think we need to launch a national campaign, national PSA, that really talks about the benefits of vaccination, because I'd be very, very concerned if we did get a [vaccine] and then we had a problem with actual adoption.

After working through all the logistics of who actually was a frontline worker and would receive the vaccine first, a surge of teammates was lining up. But then . . . we stalled.

Throughout the spring, President Biden had been pushing the Fourth of July holiday as a benchmark for getting the pandemic under control, with the nation back on track and able to safely gather to celebrate America's 245th birthday.

As vaccinations slowed, I created a task force to set our goals by Independence Day—which had double meaning: our nation's freedom and freedom from COVID-19. We decided ultimately that we would strive for one million shots in arms, including having seven out of ten teammates vaccinated by July 4. We had aimed high throughout the pandemic, and we weren't going to stop now.

In the end, we came in just shy of our goal, but we vaccinated four times the number of teammates we were originally targeting. Unfortunately, newly emerging variants of the virus made it clear that we would not be celebrating independence from COVID-19 on Independence Day. We realized that we would have no choice but to mandate that all teammates be fully vaccinated as a requisite for continued employment. And we knew that would be anything but an easy decision to implement, given the emotions tied to it and the fact that we were experiencing a staffing shortage. But it was the necessary thing to do, to keep teammates and patients safe.

Immediately after we announced the mandate, I was receiving hundreds of "anti-vax" emails weekly.

Here Come the Delta Blues

In midsummer 2021, the Delta variant descended on North Carolina like a tornado. The state reported a huge surge of the highly contagious virus, with more than 1,100 coronavirus hospitalizations, the highest total since springtime. Governor Cooper announced that more than 90 percent of those people were unvaccinated. "[They're] driving this resurgence and getting themselves and other people sick," he told the news organizations.[2] In Mecklenburg County alone, Atrium Health facilities were seeing 175 new COVID-19 cases per day. They were filling up our already overflowing emergency departments.

"We're getting pounded with very sick people," Dr. Callaway told me. "We're short on nursing staff, and we have patients in the ED waiting for ICU beds."

We were prepared to once again turn off elective surgeries and non-time-sensitive procedures, to shift beds and resources to where they were needed most. And we did. It helped, but these triage measures couldn't put out all of the fires. A COVID-19 patient uses an ICU bed not for a day or two but for weeks, sometimes three or more. And the patient in that bed needs 24/7 critical nurse care.

Technicians, equipment, doctors, nurses, physical therapists, housekeeping staff—all aspects of hospital operations and resources—were being pushed to their limits. Teammates were exhausted. Stress and burnout were at a tipping point.

I recall visiting our COVID-19 ICUs early in the pandemic in 2020 and seeing very elderly patients who appeared lifeless, hooked up to machines and alone in the hospital room, because we couldn't risk exposing their family members and spreading the disease. It was terribly sad. Many were the age of my eighty-year-old mother. But rounding the units in 2021 was different. Rather than just the elderly, I saw patients in their forties and fifties. I knew something had shifted. One battle-hardened ICU manager told me, with a look of utter exhaustion and a bit of despair in her eyes, "I wish we could actually bring the TV crews in here, so that people could see what really happens if they don't take the vaccine and mask up."

And some patients came in demanding to receive unproven treatments they had heard about on TV, such as hydroxychloroquine, which randomized trials had proven to be ineffective. Nonetheless, the clinical teams fought for every patient's life as if each one was a family member. And each unit had their own way of honoring those who died and those who made it through. One unit had a wall full of stars for every patient who "graduated" from the ICU—which was also a ray of hope for the new patients being wheeled in.

President Biden announced vaccination requirements for federal government workers in July and called on the private sector to do more to encourage vaccinations as well. We decided to play a lead role, by coordinating with other health systems, to make our announcement through the North Carolina Hospital Association. The move drew a swift response from fifty-five Republican members of the North Carolina House of Representatives, in a letter to me and the CEOs of Novant Health, Duke University Health System, Cone Health, Wake Forest Baptist Health, and UNC Health. They said that while they understood it was well within our rights to mandate the vaccine, they encouraged us to reexamine the requirement, calling it unfair to "force . . . healthcare heroes serving on the frontlines against COVID-19 to choose between their job and taking a vaccine that is only authorized for emergency use." They also warned that "a hospital could lose 30% of its workforce due to vaccine mandates." We clearly knew the risk of losing staff by mandating the vaccine. We had already experienced nursing staff shortages due to the overtime demands of treating surge after surge of COVID-19 patients. Burnout had reached epic proportions, and many nurses and doctors began to retire early or just quit, to pursue other, less stressful careers.

"During the first year of COVID-19, people looked at us as healthcare heroes," recalled Maureen Swick, then our chief nursing officer. "People were bringing us food, cheering us on. But when we started to mandate the vaccine to protect our patients and team, the tone began to shift."

Delta brought a wave of very sick people spilling into our hospitals. With ambulatory offices reopened, we lost that pool of nurses, so we had quite a bit of turnover.

Swick said our nursing supervisors were doing everything in their power to hire more registered nurses (RNs) and licensed practical nurses (LPNs), offering signing bonuses, flexible hours, and premium pay for hard-to-fill shifts. The shortages were not only impacting nursing; we also saw shortages of phlebotomy and lab staff, clinical techs, and respiratory therapists.

The situation was dire, and it was nationwide. So, we clearly understood the risk of the mandate, but to paraphrase Dr. King, we felt the true measure of our system was not going to be measured by easy decisions but the decisions we made in the face of "challenge and controversy." We decided to set a deadline for all employees to be fully vaccinated by October 31 or provide an approved medical or religious exemption. Otherwise, they would not be able to work for us any longer.

And Then the Protests Began

On Sunday, August 1, 2021, roughly 700 people, including approximately 100 healthcare workers, marched from Charlotte's Freedom Park to our main medical center, carrying signs that read "Fauci Lied!" "I'm Not Your Lab Rat!" and "Freedom to Choose." The protestors chanted, "No vax mandate! I'm no guinea pig!"

The protests were mostly peaceful, but its participants were very vocal. One of the protestors who seemed especially vocal was one of our own—and was recognized by our team immediately. I was unequivocal in my direction to the team. Unless someone was violent or broke the law, there would be no retaliation of any kind for those who marched and expressed their First Amendment rights.

We anticipated early that there would be teammates who would disagree with the vaccine requirement—although the annual flu shot was a condition of employment for similar reasons: to keep our teammates and patients safe. But we recognized that this was a novel situation. We understood that our organization is a microcosm of the United States, with people from all walks of life and with a wide range of views. This very large family reflects what we've seen in our own families—sometimes passionately divergent opinions that can test the fabric of love that holds us together.

But especially following George Floyd's murder, we knew how critical it was to create safe spaces for courageous conversations when people had different experiences and views.

One emergency department nurse wrote to me when we announced our vaccine requirement, saying, "There's not enough evidence of safety; I don't want to be a guinea pig." I responded by letting her know I understood her concerns, and I asked if she would be willing to speak with Dr.

Passaretti to discuss the clinical safety studies that had been conducted. She agreed, and she ultimately received the vaccine.

Another teammate wrote, "If our patients can choose to not vaccinate, so should we." Another commented: "My body is my body, not Atrium's."

Another teammate I ran into outside of work told me she loved her job but had decided to retire early because of our mandate. "It's not the vaccine," she said, "it's the principle; it's about our freedom and our right to choose."

I told her I truly appreciated her tremendous service and shared that while I understood her perspective, I believed that patients coming into our hospitals had a right to know their caregivers were not going to be the ones to give them COVID-19. The encounter reminded me of a conversation I had with my youngest son, who at first chose not to wear a mask because he wasn't worried about catching the virus—and thought if he did become sick, he was young enough to fight it. We talked about how he felt, and I explained that wearing a mask wasn't just about his protection but for that of his friends, his family, and his grandmother. That made sense to him immediately, and then he became extraordinarily strict about wearing his mask. He was never around me without one.

The national polls were telling us early that white Republican men and African Americans were the cohorts most likely to be reluctant to get the vaccine. And it was for basically the same reason—lack of trust in institutions. Some doubted the science. For many African Americans, reluctance and fear stemmed in part from the horrors of the forty-year Tuskegee Experiment, the unethical study conducted by the United States Public Health Service, beginning in 1932, that gave 400 Black men diagnosed with syphilis sham or placebo treatments in order for scientists to study the untreated progression of the disease. Study participants were told they were being treated for "bad blood" but were never given any treatment despite the fact that penicillin could effectively treat syphilis. National acknowledgment of the enormous tragedy to the countless families affected would not come until 1997, when President Bill Clinton issued a formal presidential apology.

We saw those issues of trust play out daily, and we worked hard to craft targeted messages tailored to specific audiences. Often there was no better spokesperson than the patient who had spent weeks on a ventilator near death in one of our intensive-care units. Many of these people became passionate advocates, back in their own communities, because they had experienced firsthand that this was truly about life or death.

I, too, found myself fielding questions about vaccine safety from my own extended family members. I shared how disturbing it was to see the suffering of ICU patients dealing with COVID-19. It starts with intubation, in which we put a breathing tube down a patient's throat and attach them to a ventilator to support their breathing. This is something we do routinely for operations and in recovery. For the short term, it's very safe and effective, but during long-term use for COVID-19 care, which could be for several weeks or longer, the mechanical breathing can result in complications and can also lead to extreme anxiety.

"Intubation is never like the way you breathe normally," said registered respiratory therapist Chad Harvey, MHA. "We're pushing air in, and you're breathing it back out. That process is not very comfortable at all."

Notwithstanding all the misinformation circulating during the Delta surge, we knew we needed to keep at it. Our goal was to build trust, not villainize those who did not want to get the vaccine, and we wanted to send a consistent message based on science and our day-to-day clinical experience.

We doubled down on our social media efforts and enlisted the help of faith leaders and other voices in the community to spread the word. We tracked the polling data and created different messages for different messengers to deliver to their constituents. We even found that some people who had changed their minds about being vaccinated were afraid to do so publicly and risk being ostracized in their social circles. So, we began encouraging the community to get the vaccine privately during routine checkups with their family doctors.

In our own organization, we took a similar grassroots approach, expressing honestly that we wanted teammates vaccinated for their own good, for the good of their families, and because we had an obligation to keep our patients safe. While some of the politicians fanned the flames of division, we tried to match the anger and sometimes vitriol with kindness and love. Our teammates are like our family, after all, and we wanted to make it clear that we wanted the best for them, even if they decided to leave or refused to be vaccinated and faced being let go. To that end, we launched a major face-to-face effort to listen and share information. We trained our frontline leaders and staff to have conversations—to, as Ted Lasso puts it, "Be curious, not judgmental." We strove to establish bonds, rather than engage in countering conspiracy theories.

Five weeks before our October 31 deadline for all employees to be fully vaccinated, there were still 22,000 who had not yet gotten the shot. We had our work cut out for us. Some teammates were holding out, thinking it unlikely that our organization would follow through on its promise to terminate staff who didn't comply with the vaccine mandate. We were making daily progress and understood the severe challenges if we lost thousands of frontline teammates on November 1. But we also couldn't blink. We mapped out scenarios to prepare for multiple contingencies. In one scenario that was considered the most probable, we'd lose 2,000 teammates. That would be very difficult, but the team had mapped out how to consolidate units, cross cover, and implement backup plans to still be able to operate to care for patients 24/7.

At the same time, we went to extraordinary lengths to engage with those who were still on the fence about the vaccine. We told those who didn't want to comply with the vaccine policy that we would help with their job search assistance, with resume-building and interviewing skills seminars, and retraining for those who wanted to pursue employment in other fields.

In summer 2021, the Biden administration implemented policies requiring federal employees and federal contractors to be vaccinated. By the fall, the Department of Health and Human Services announced its requirement that healthcare workers at facilities participating in Medicare and Medicaid be fully vaccinated. After battling this as a health system, we appreciated the government following suit on the requirement, because it would help our efforts. Even private businesses employing more than 100 people would be required to issue mandates.

Our plan paid off. More than 99 percent of our 70,000-person work-force became fully vaccinated. We ended up transitioning approximately

300 employees; we were sad to see them go and wished them well. We had successfully navigated this battle just in time, as an even more transmissible variant—Omicron—began to assert its dominance throughout the world.

CHAPTER 3

The "Why" of What We Do

By the beginning of 2022, the number of lives taken by COVID-19 in the United States had surpassed 800,000. It was a shocking milestone. And yet it was clear that people were becoming desensitized to pandemic statistics, a psychological phenomenon known as psychic numbing. Most people care about one individual at a time, but when large numbers come into play, people can begin to lose sensitivity and emotional connectivity. The trauma of 800,000 dying and the impact that it had on their loved ones is hard to take in, versus knowing a specific friend who came down with COVID-19.

So psychic numbing was something we needed to guard against. We have many millions of patient interactions every year. Each one of those is a human being, with their own story, who has come to us for help. We are their shoulder to cry on and hand to hold during the best and worst days of their lives.

That is why I started a tradition called Connect to Purpose. Before every meeting, including board meetings, we tell a story about how we helped heal a patient or how we lifted up a fellow teammate. It grounds us in the "why" of what we do and breaks it down into the impact we have on people, one life at a time.

Many times, teammates also share personal stories about how a healthcare experience has affected their lives and the lives of those they love. I'm sure it's not difficult for you to recall a time when someone close to you was very sick or dying and how it made you feel. For me, it's very easy. Though I was very young at the time, I remember a family tragedy that impacted me profoundly. I share this story here because it influenced my interest in pursuing a career in the health field, and I'm sure many of my colleagues can recall similar experiences that launched their passions for selflessly serving people in need.

My Aunt Carmen

This story begins in southern Spain, where I spent most of my early childhood. My mother, Maria, is Spanish, from the town of Jerez de la Frontera, a bustling city in the Andalusia region. My father, Eugene, was from rural Tennessee. He met Mom when he was a U.S. sailor at Naval Station Rota, the Spanish-American base in the province of Cádiz, not far from Jerez.

I went to the American school on the naval base, from kindergarten through fourth grade. It was a cool place for a boy. I remember being fascinated by the submarines and ships from the U.S. Sixth Fleet in the Mediterranean Sea, especially those enormous aircraft carriers. When docked at Rota, they looked capable of pulling the entire base into the Bay of Cádiz. My father, a navy aircraft mechanic, would take me to see the military transport planes he worked on: the huge C-5 Galaxy; the C-141 Starlifter, which sent vibrations through your body on takeoff; and the awkward-looking Marine UH-34 Seahorse helicopters. I remember thinking that if it wasn't for my dad, those copters would crash into the sea. The man could fix anything, from complicated aeronautic systems to anyone's VW Bug on base.

When I wasn't in school, I spent most of my days at my grandparents' home, a ground-floor flat in Jerez. Their apartment couldn't have been much larger than 900 square feet, and they lived there with their twelve children. It was always cozy (i.e., crowded) and loud, with robust debates on what soccer team was better—Real Madrid or Barcelona. And it felt as if someone was always on the verge of breaking out a flamenco song or dance. It was a culturally rich and fun way to grow up. Family was everything.

When I was entering fifth grade, though, Dad was reassigned to Pennsylvania, to Naval Air Development Center Warminster, in the suburbs between Philadelphia and Trenton. My parents tried to sell me on the new adventure and the new base we would move to. It was famous for being the site of the world's largest human centrifuge. Back in the fifties and sixties, the massive Tilt-o-Whirl whipped around astronauts like John Glenn and Neil Armstrong, to train them for the effects of g-forces while piloting rockets.

I had all the trepidation you might expect from a ten-year-old. And I didn't want to leave my big Spanish family. I also knew of the racial unrest in the United States, which I had seen on television. I felt it in my bones that I would be stepping into the unknown, where the color of my skin would be a factor in how people engaged with me.

My Aunt Carmen must have sensed my anxiety in the weeks leading up to our departure. She was amazing, always attuned to others' feelings. Carmen was the wife of my Uncle Augustín, the second eldest of my mom's seven brothers. Aunt Carmen knew I loved music. So, as a going-away present, she gave me my very first record album, Simon & Garfunkel's *Greatest Hits*. I'm sure she thought the album would ease the transition to the States, or at least to American music, which was so unlike the flamenco that constantly played in my grandparents' home. It did. There was something uniquely comforting about the song "America," which I began to play nonstop.

Looking back, I will always remember Aunt Carmen's acts of caring. Even as a child, it felt like she was not only elegant and beautiful in a Jacqueline Kennedy Onassis way but was also one of the kindest souls you could ever meet. She was beloved by everyone. I was an altar boy, and I thought she embodied the qualities of the Mary I knew from my catechism.

Though she rarely let on, Carmen suffered from debilitating headaches for many years. She had been to countless doctors without relief. In 1980, I was fifteen years old, and my mom, dad, sister, and I were living in Warminster when Uncle Augustín called to say that Aunt Carmen had entered a hospital in Seville, about one hour north of Jerez, for tests and treatment.

Carmen was in a semiprivate room with an elderly woman next to her by the window, and she had quickly become a favorite of the nurses on her hospital floor, because of the interest she showed in *their* lives.

Despite her terrible migraines, she even helped the nurses care for the elderly woman who shared her hospital room. Aunt Carmen brushed the woman's white hair in the evenings. She helped her to the restroom in the middle of the night. Sadly, the elderly woman passed away in her sleep a few days after Carmen's arrival. The nurses wanted to do something nice for Carmen and moved her to be near the window, so she could enjoy the view of the city.

That evening, a new shift of nurses came onto Carmen's floor and began medication rounds. Shortly after Carmen took the drugs, she began to have severe abdominal pains. Uncle Augustín was in the room with her. He helped her to the bathroom, but she had a seizure in the doorway and collapsed unconscious in his arms. Augustín called for the nurses, who tried to revive her as doctors rushed in.

But she was gone. The beautiful mother of three young children was gone.

The cause of death? A medication error. The nurses on the evening shift had given Carmen the medicine indicated for the patient in bed number two, the one near the window. Carmen had been issued the elderly woman's pills by mistake, and it was what caused the seizure that stopped her heart.

I was doing homework in my room when my mother came in to tell me the news. I don't remember crying, just experiencing a profound sense of sadness.

I couldn't concentrate on my math homework. I remember putting on a song by Simon & Garfunkel, who had then become one of my favorite artists, called "Bridge Over Troubled Water."

> When you're weary
> Feeling small
> When tears are in your eyes
> I'll dry them all
> I'm on your side

Aunt Carmen's death had a profound impact on me. While I may not have fully realized it at the time, it planted seeds in my psyche. Doctors, nurses, and hospitals were mysteries, but I couldn't contemplate how a mistake like that could even occur, and what it would take to ensure no other mistakes would result in the loss of a loved one like Carmen. I was a rather idealistic teenager who thought he could somehow "save" the world. And I remember feeling that being of some sort of service to others would honor my Aunt Carmen. I just didn't know how, at least not until I entered college, and my path forward started to become clear.

Inviting Serendipity

I believe we are cocreators in serendipity. Things in life happen for a reason, as the saying goes, but the adventure we are all on requires being open to embracing life's unexpected twists and turns.

When high school graduation came around, all I knew was that I intended to be the first in my family to get a college degree—though I had little idea what I wanted to be. And my public school guidance counselor wasn't particularly helpful even on how to apply to schools. I remember one suggesting I go into a two-year vocational school or join the military like my dad did. I respected those professions, but I knew they weren't for me. I wanted to carve out a different path but didn't know what. Neither of my parents were college-educated, so they couldn't advise me if they wanted to. I was on my own.

During my senior year, I worked at the local Acme grocery store after school and on weekends. I remember being taken aside by a fellow worker as the shift was ending. He seemed very old at the time, and in retrospect he was probably in his forties. He said, "Hey kid, make sure you do well in college and figure out what you want to do, because, trust me, you don't want to be stuck here working for the next twenty years, stocking shelves like I have. You have the ability to aspire to much bigger things."

So, I ended up applying to one of Penn State University's branch campuses, called Penn State Ogontz, in Abington, just a few miles down the road from Warminster. I needed to be close to home, because my parents had recently divorced. Mom had to go to work for the first time in her life, and my sister Maria was still in high school, so I felt obligated to stay nearby to help, as the man of the household.

After my first year at Ogontz, I experienced one of those fortuitous accidents in life that resulted in me finding the career I would dedicate my life to. When I mentioned to a trusted professor that I was having trouble selecting a major, he suggested I attend a career session on international business the following week.

After ten minutes, I wondered when the gentleman leading the session was going to mention international business. The speaker explained that his industry was going through a huge transformation, and it needed bright, young minds. He said his work was extremely rewarding. "This is a profession where you have tremendous opportunities to change lives and the course of communities for the better." It was then I realized that the speaker was the CEO of the local hospital. I had mixed up my days and wandered into a discussion about Penn State's healthcare administration major by mistake!

After the session, I waited until the crowd had filed out, and I asked the hospital exec some questions. He told me he felt his was one of the few careers where you could apply what you learned in business school to serve people every day.

I knew immediately that I had found my career. The next day, I decided to pursue a degree in healthcare planning and administration. The uncertainty I'd been feeling during that summer after graduating from high school was replaced with a real sense of direction and purpose. I began excelling in the classes I took. I transferred to Penn State's main campus in State College the following fall, when I felt the situation at home was stable, and eventually became president of the health planning and administration (HPA) student club, working with Dr. Stanley Mayers, who had helped found the HPA department. I committed to doing everything in my power when I graduated to try to prevent tragedies like the one that took my Aunt Carmen. It fueled my energy and passion to learn everything I could. I later came to fully believe that there are no accidents in the universe. I was destined for a career in healthcare.

CHAPTER 4

Improvisation: Leading through Crisis

The experience of stepping into a vocation by stepping into the wrong lecture hall initiated my education into improvisation. At every stop along my career path, I learned that a hospital executive plays multiple roles, like a musician. At times the role requires you to be an orchestra conductor, because you have to make sure the whole band is playing on time and in harmony, with the precision of Bach's *Brandenburg Concertos*. On the other hand, though, the role requires you to let go of playing a prewritten score and approach leadership like a jazz musician who plays and flows with the rhythms of the ever-changing moment. Miles Davis once said, "Composing will always be a memory of inspiration; improvising is live inspiration, something happening at that very moment. Do not fear mistakes. There are none."

As a musician who has played guitar for over fifty years, my work as a healthcare leader always reminded me of leading and performing in bands, as I did in my college days. To play jazz or blues guitar means learning to be comfortable with improvisation, going off-script, and taking an intuitive leap into the unknown, while always staying in the present. Likewise, a hospital executive learns he or she must react strategically to what's happening in the moment and problem-solve creatively while ensuring that everyone is playing in concert with the precision and accuracy that will prevent tragic errors.

The art of leadership is knowing when you should play which role. Sometimes, healthcare requires you lead as the conductor of a classical symphony. But as we came to experience during the pandemic, it's often unpredictable, spontaneous, even messy at times, in the way jazz can *seem* messy. And managing through the pandemic had an analogous feel. It came with no playbook. It was all-new territory, and we were forced to improvise and adapt in real time and make decisions with imperfect information and rapidly evolving dynamics. But that's often where creativity and innovation can shine, and you can do your best work if you embrace the ambiguity.

Figuring It Out on the Fly

I learned early in my career that when you're faced with a monumental challenge and striving to enroll people in large-scale change, there's power in articulating a compelling narrative to the audience from whom you hope to gain trust. It's about communicating in a way that meets people where they are—and not using what I call "administrative speak." It's about cutting through confusion and explaining the most compelling "why" of an issue. And often, as CEO, that means starting with your why.

In the late 1990s, I was hired by a small hospital, Roy L. Schneider Hospital, in St. Thomas, in the U.S. Virgin Islands. I was in my early thirties, and to this day it is one of the toughest jobs I have ever had. To say that island politics is rough-and-tumble is an understatement. The operation of the hospitals in the U.S. Virgin Islands was tightly controlled by a well-entrenched government. The hospitals had no autonomy to handle their own finances, personnel, and procurement. It made operating effectively nearly impossible. It was like having both hands tied behind our backs as we tried to give our caregivers the tools they needed to serve the needs of the territory. I could write an entire new book about the challenges I ended up leading through.

For example, I received a phone call from my laboratory director, late one Friday afternoon, only a few weeks into my new job. It was Mr. Turnbull, who asked if he could come to my office to visit in person. He was a physically imposing man, over six feet five inches tall, but with a gentle demeanor. He told me that our emergency department had just received a kid with a gunshot wound. He needed a lot of blood, but our supply was being depleted, especially because we had other patients in the ICUs going through our supply fast as well. Turnbull said he feared we wouldn't have enough blood inventory to last us the weekend.

I had never encountered a situation like that before. But I knew the lives of these patients would depend on whether I made the right next decisions—and I had hours, not days, to figure it out. The off-island blood bank refused to send more until we settled our outstanding bill, which was owed not by the hospital but by the government. And we at the hospital didn't have the authority to write our own checks.

I immediately called the finance official of the Health Board and explained the dire situation.

"Your team hasn't completed the necessary paperwork," she responded in a dispassionately bureaucratic voice.

"I promise I will look at that first thing on Monday," I responded, "but right now we have an emergency."

"Yeah, well, it's Friday afternoon, and my check writers have gone home," she countered.

I was incredulous. *Really?* I thought to myself. *Lives are at stake and you are talking about paperwork?*

I took a deep breath to maintain my emotional control and said, "Then I need you to understand that if these patients do not make it, it is my obligation to share the content of our conversation today with the families of the patients . . . and we would have a responsibility to disclose with any regulatory body that would no doubt investigate." I added that I was sending a courier over immediately to pick up the check, even if she was the one to have to write it herself. I knew I had to take an unequivocal stand, and the check soon arrived.

Late that evening, lifesaving blood arrived by plane.

The valuable lesson I learned is that systems left to their own natural tendencies, without direct interventions, can result in failing the very people they intend to serve. I won that skirmish, but the battle continued. Some of the island politicians initially saw me as a "state-sider," a young upstart who had come to make waves and wrestle power away from the government. They eventually realized that my motivations were quite simple—to turn that hospital system into one where I would feel comfortable sending my family for care. That is still my guiding principle.

That experience prompted me to push for changes to the laws governing hospitals, and I recall sitting down with one of the senators, Allie Petrus, who encouraged me to draft what would become the basis for the new law granting hospitals semi-autonomy from core government functions. The goal was to remove the bureaucratic shackles and empower us to do what was needed to recruit new physicians, install new systems, buy state-of-the-art equipment to replace that which was well beyond its useful life, and to begin to make repairs on the hospital that was still damaged by previous hurricanes. We were losing millions in revenue to mainland U.S. hospitals, as people left the territory for treatment rather than find care on the islands. That had long-term implications for the survivability of the only hospital on St. Thomas itself.

The fundamental challenge ahead of me was to articulate the set of very complex changes that needed to be made to the people of the Virgin Islands and the government bureaucrats. I quickly learned the essence of grassroots political success: telling a compelling story. It requires being versed in the type of storytelling that truly resonates with people, in a way that they can understand how it affects them personally. I had a knowing sense that our policymakers and citizens simply didn't understand how our institution was run and how the laws that hamstrung our operation trickled down and directly impacted the people we were trying to serve.

So, I went on live TV to tell the story. I used as an example one of the most fundamental requirements of any hospital in caring for people that come to us daily for lifesaving care—an adequate supply of blood. I walked the community on live TV through our blood procurement process, step by step, to illustrate how vendors were cutting us off from critical supplies because we didn't have the authority to pay our own bills. It was show-and-tell time. Whenever we needed a piece of critical equipment, I explained, we had to present justification to the Health Department, where it would languish for months and even years. And we didn't have that time; we had dialysis machines, for example, that were on their last legs. Hiring desperately needed positions, such as doctors, lab techs, nurses, and pharmacists, would take many, many months as well. And we were being forced to hire traveler nurses at a premium to fill our needs.

I had to make it crystal clear that we were not attempting to circumvent the oversight responsibility of the government but rather to streamline a cumbersome process—so that when they or a loved one came to us for care, we would have the tools and supplies we needed.

My narrative had to hit home. But I also had to be careful to avoid frightening the public. It boiled down to delivering a message about the critical nature of the current situation but also offering a prospection for a better future. Make it about something everyone knows is essential—such as blood—and everyone can get it, thinking, *I don't want my family to end up at the hospital where there's no blood.*

The many battles I had in St. Thomas were formative for me. The challenges helped me understand just how critical the laws and regulations, whether at the state capitol or on Capitol Hill, are to delivering quality care and access—and that they could be a big impediment or an enabler. And I understood that, for a healthcare executive to provide truly the best care possible, I could not stay inside of my walls. I had to directly engage with community and the political establishment. It was this insight in my thirties that eventually led me to join the American Hospital Association Board—ultimately becoming chair of the principal advocacy organization for nearly 5,000 hospitals and healthcare systems nationwide.

Ultimately we succeeded, after many public hearings, to pass the USVI Public Hospitals Semi-Autonomy Act. And it provided immediate relief. But it wasn't a panacea. The work of building new systems and processes was as challenging as passing the new law. But we were committed, because we knew that the island and those who visited were counting on us.

The Obstacle Is the Way

The core element for communicating effectively in a tough negotiation, as Stephen Covey would say, is listening to understand first, and then speaking to be understood. Done well, these things are foundational to establishing the most critical element of trust.

When you and the party with which you are negotiating are speaking the same language, as the saying goes, you are more likely to come to a resolution. Like a songwriter's lyrics, if your words influence people's perspective, allowing the listeners to hear things differently, you can make progress.

You have to stay open to the music as it plays. That's where breakthroughs occur in negotiations, where parties begin dialoguing on a new level that reveals solutions to their stalemates.

When I was chief operating officer of CHRISTUS Health, a Catholic faith-based, not-for-profit health system in Irving, Texas, I was tasked with diversifying the organization and repositioning it internationally. At one point, we were entrenched in challenging negotiations with a family with whom we were joint-venture partners in a group of hospitals in Mexico. We were reworking the incorporation documents, to give CHRISTUS majority control for managing the twelve-hospital organization, so it could operate more effectively and better serve the communities there. The negotiations were extraordinarily intense. I recall many trips to Monterrey for meetings, with the airport filled with Mexican police and national guardsmen. They carried automatic weapons and wore masks to avoid being identified by the drug cartels. In fact, shortly before I joined CHRISTUS, a foe of the drug lords was found hanged by the neck from a bridge in Monterrey, wearing a sign in Spanish that read, "The monster has arrived."

The backdrop of chaos and fear in Monterrey seemed to infuse the mood of the meetings. They got intense. The family owners had strong connections to the Sisters of Charity of the Incarnate Word in San Antonio, which had helped to found CHRISTUS Santa Rosa in the late 1800s. The family began trying to circumvent the process, upset by the negotiations. I knew I needed an ally that they respected and trusted, so I met with the sisters and asked one of the leading nuns to be CHRISTUS's chair of the board in Mexico. Who better to make the family feel comfortable than a sister with the moral authority to help them understand that what we were proposing was in keeping with furthering the mission of the sisters' health ministry?

Sister Teresa Maya was exactly the right person at the right time. She was smart, charismatic, and trusted to do the right thing by all parties. But she was also tough, which went a long way toward advancing the arduous negotiations.

The fact that I spoke fluent Spanish ultimately helped as well—as I held the negotiations in Spanish, which could often get quite loud. In a way, I felt right at home; the negotiations were characteristic of the Spanish debates I grew up with at my grandparents' home in Jerez de la Frontera, Spain. At one point, the lead negotiator, Fernando, the family's trusted friend, pounded his fist on the table and yelled at me.

"Do not speak to Mr. Woods in that tone!" countered one of our lawyers.

I laughed and said, "It's all right. How about the lawyers leave the room so I can talk to Fernando privately?"

My team wasn't familiar with that kind of negotiation. But I knew it wasn't personal. I took no offense at all. Behind closed doors, Fernando and I worked out some fine points of the deal in Spanish, sometimes raising our voices to make a point, but little by little we worked through a mutually acceptable deal.

We sealed the deal with a handshake, and Fernando decided to ask someone to take a picture on his iPhone to memorialize the moment. A couple of weeks later, when we had inked the documents, a copy of that photo arrived in my office with a note from Fernando written in Spanish: *de un hijo de puta a otro.* "From one son of a bitch to another." It was his humorous way of saying that I had earned his respect and an acknowledgment that we had done right by not just the family but the community.

In a favorite book of mine, *The Obstacle Is the Way*, author Ryan Holiday writes, "The obstacle in the path becomes the path. Never forget, within every obstacle is an opportunity to improve." I've come to realize that in everything important and worth doing, there will always be obstacles, occasions to learn a few new guitar licks in leadership.

That sums up the responsibility of leadership—to improve the human condition within the organizational mission you serve. And to not bemoan the inevitable obstacles, but instead to embrace them as necessary to making this a better society.

That said, overcoming obstacles always requires significant doses of grit, improvisation, teamwork, passion, and vision.

Letting Others Solo

The fastest way to grow as a leader is to successfully lead people through a disaster. I learned that in one of my first executive roles a few years out of grad school. I was hired as vice president of administration at Southside Regional Medical Center in Petersburg, Virginia, and was tasked with bringing a troubled hospital back on track.

When I arrived, Southside Regional was on the verge of losing its accreditation license. I mounted an effort that had us receive the highest marks the hospital had ever had in its history. In the process, I got to learn the inner workings of the system and gain the trust of the team— most importantly the CEO. Then an even greater crisis struck.

It was New Year's Eve, 1994. A patient with behavioral health issues had to be placed in temporary restraints when she became upset at being denied a cigarette inside the hospital, where smoking is prohibited. Somehow the patient's friend managed to sneak her a cigarette when the nurses were out of the room—and the patient got an arm free when she left and lit up. Investigators concluded that a dropped match or cigarette embers ignited a fire. Melted oxygen lines rapidly fueled the blaze into an inferno. The fire consumed the fourth floor of the 448-bed hospital, killing four patients and injuring twenty. A fifth patient died a short time later.

It was a terrible accident, and the loss of life was unbearable for the entire hospital community. But we had a responsibility to explore the causes of the tragedy and learn from the investigation so it would never ever happen again.

Investigators from the state health department, the National Fire Protection Association, and a national hospital accrediting group questioned us rigorously. Our CEO put me in charge of managing the inquiry and organizing our response. It was the first time in my career that I had been given that kind of responsibility. He was taking a chance on my ability to help lead us through the crisis. The consequences of failing to do so would be losing our license and Medicare funding—which would have effectively shut down the hospital. And the experience taught me some valuable lessons. First, to trust the people you've hired to do their jobs. In a band—jazz, rock, whatever—every player has a part. It's the same for businesses and organizations; often the leader needs to sit out for a bit and let someone else take a lead solo. My CEO showed confidence in me by letting me run the show without playing the second-guessing game. That gave *me* the confidence to trust my instincts when I needed them most.

Secondly, it groomed me to become what I call a "cloud-to-ground" leader. The gravity of the responsibility given to me in the aftermath of the tragic fire forced me to be hyper-focused on detail. On the flip side, you can't let that ground-level perspective make you lose sight of the larger goal. In this case, the goal was to keep this hospital viable, which was so important to the community. And then there's this idea of calm under pressure: a leader needs to demonstrate to the organization that he can navigate through the choppiest of waters—because that, in and of itself, inspires confidence. The more complicated things get, the more centered and grounded you must become. It's not projecting false confidence but demonstrating a realistic optimism that broadcasts to your team, "Hey, we may not know everything we need to know, but we'll figure this out; we've got this."

This all starts with fully understanding the current reality with brutal honesty about the facts. I needed to get on the ground and understand healthcare's complex regulatory environment, to be able to carve a path out of the quagmire.

The health department's investigation of the fire at one point became extremely frustrating. They were asking us to supply information that had nothing to do with the details of the tragedy. It was easy to get defensive at that line of inquiry, but I had to project a sense of calm and redirect them to the safety measures we were putting in place to ensure something like this never happened again. I had to humanize the narrative, to show them how seriously we were taking the process and how deeply the loss of life affected the entire staff. And it did traumatize our people terribly. Many struggled with feelings of guilt, even though they had responded heroically. I shared that our nurses didn't run from the fire but to it, crawling on hands and knees under the thick smoke to make sure the patients were safely out of harm's way and then going back in to get the patients' charts. We were much more paper-oriented back in those days; the nurses risked their lives so we wouldn't lose those critical medical records. That picture of how our staff responded in the danger of the moment helped to reframe the investigating committee's thinking, so that they comprehended that this is what our people do; this is how much they care.

After months of meetings with regulators, we retained our accreditation and were able to move on and rebuild. We implemented significant changes to safety procedures to ensure a tragedy like this never happened again.

For me, it was a lesson in how to lead. My CEO gave me that golden opportunity for real career and personal growth, to enhance those skills that would serve me down the road. He knew when to allow another band member to solo. You know, sometimes you need to be a lead guitarist like Jimi Hendrix, setting the tone for the entire song. But sometimes the drummer needs to be the one to step up and hold the band together from the back.

A Day Like No Other
Code Orange!

It seemed like something out of a movie or one of those hospital series on TV. You know, where you hear someone shout, "Code blue!" and suddenly the doctors run off to save a patient in cardiac arrest.

It was my fourth day on the job over operations at Medstar Washington Center Hospital in Washington, D.C. I was sitting in the basement auditorium for a hospital orientation meeting when the presentation was interrupted, ironically shortly after the presentation on managing disaster and mass casualty incidents. The announcement over the loudspeakers blasted "Code Orange. This is Not a Drill. Code Orange. This is not a drill." Over and over. The presenter had just reviewed the hospital's color code system for identifying different types of emergencies, and at Washington Hospital Center, code orange meant: implement disaster preparedness protocols.

People started running out of the auditorium toward their stations.

The day was September 11, 2001.

Code Orange meant that the terror we had just learned was unfolding in New York City had come to D.C. A passenger jet had crashed into the Pentagon, a few miles southwest of the hospital across the Potomac in Arlington.

I started making my way back to my new office and became disoriented. Washington Center was a massive, almost 1,000-bed complex, but I didn't want to ask for directions. It was not the kind of thing that would inspire staff confidence in the new COO. But I got my bearings and made it to my office.

Our Medstar helicopter was the first to touch down on the scene at the Pentagon. *My God*, I thought. *What happened at the towers in New York just happened here. We're going to get flooded with patients.*

I took a deep breath, grabbed the orange disaster manual from the bookshelf, and sat down. I took ten minutes to try to orient myself with this new organization I'd been a part of for just a few days and prepare for meetings to assess our response and needs.

We had a very comprehensive air ambulance group and the largest burn unit in the region, with two of the top burn trauma surgeons in the country. It wouldn't be long before we would start receiving the most critically injured survivors.

One of our medical helicopters almost got shot down. The Air Force had scrambled fighter jets to shoot down any aircraft in D.C. airspace that couldn't be vetted, and our choppers didn't have identifier numbers, so it made for some tense moments as our pilots tried to explain who they were. Ultimately, our medical helicopters were allowed to pick up the wounded to take them to the hospital.

We also quickly learned that the feds on-site considered Washington Hospital Center and the surrounding medical campuses, which included a children's hospital and the VA hospital, to be likely targets for terrorists if more attacks on D.C. were planned. All of this elevated the anxiety of emergency staff as they awaited the arrival of casualties on the helipad and ambulance ramp.

Sometimes there's no better way to get to know your team and their talents quickly than to be thrown into a crisis situation. We received the ten most severely burned victims of the attack that day.

One hundred eighty-nine people perished at the Pentagon, including sixty-four on American Airlines Flight 77. Our surgeons and critical-care staff worked thirty-six-hour shifts to stabilize and then heal the burn victims—for weeks on end.

One of those Pentagon patients, Maj. David J. King Jr., arrived with his trousers melted onto his legs. His upper body fared worse, with third-degree burns. His left arm, from its fingertips to above the elbow, had to be repaired with skin grafts from his thighs and rib cage. It took four separate operations. In all, he spent five weeks at Washington Center Hospital. In an interview with the U.S. Army Center for Military History, King said he was fortunate to have been taken to Washington Hospital Center. "They [had] the best burn doctor in the country, and I'm not just saying it because he worked on me. . . . We were fortunate he was there. The nursing staff was outstanding. The rehabilitation staff, I thought at the time, was very brutal, but outstanding. They knew they had to push us."[1]

Over the months that followed September 11, as I came to know our executive team and clinicians, I witnessed the same awe-inspiring human devotion at the Washington Hospital Center that I've seen in every single health system in which I've worked before and since. Our healthcare workers are living and breathing heroes—even putting their lives on the line, just as we've seen throughout the COVID-19 pandemic. Their oath to put their patients first is something I witness every single day.

All but one of the Pentagon patients who had been horribly injured by the burning jet fuel were saved by our trauma teams at Washington Hospital Center. By Christmastime, the last of the victims left the hospital, to be reunited with their families.

Improvising amid Ambiguity

Hospitals plan for the unthinkable. Clinical staff practice emergency protocols until they can be executed with routine precision. There are systems in place to help everyone move methodically and confidently amid chaos, whether it's a cardiac patient coding or multiple gunshot victims arriving at once in the emergency department. But as famed management guru Peter Drucker once asserted, hospitals are "the most complex form of human organization we have ever attempted to manage." That's certainly been my experience at each of the hospital systems I have served. The level of complexity is onerous, and while it is important to ensure the vehicle is well-oiled and its suspension properly calibrated, the unexpected potholes are what test a car's reliability and your ability to drive safely. The pandemic made that truth clear to anyone with a television or a smartphone.

If there's any lesson to be found in the rubble of COVID-19, it's that the traditional ways of thinking and doing in medicine are inadequate. We must adopt a pioneer spirit and truly embrace improvisation to advance the evolution of healthcare—and not just talk about it.

In an uncertain world, adaptability is a competitive advantage.

CHAPTER 5

History Has Its Eyes on Us

It is my will that Grace and Ann with their families have the use of the house they now live in together with the small field lying between the stage and railroads, Grace during her lifetime and Ann for the term of fifteen years after the death of my wife upon the condition they remain with and assist my wife during her lifetime and do not disturb any family that may hereafter live at my present residence.

The last will and testament of Citizen S. Woods,
1865, Carroll County, Tennessee
(Regarding my ancestors)

Growing up in Spain, I knew my grandparents on my mother's side, the Castillas. We lived on the naval base less than ten miles from them and would visit just about every weekend. There were always stories being shared. I learned that my grandfather's father, at age sixteen, fought in the Spanish Civil War. He was wounded and, presumed dead, was transported to a makeshift morgue in a farmhouse where he regained consciousness—in a room full of soldiers killed in battle.

My mother told us the story of *her* grandfather, a farmer, who married a woman of high society. She recalled that her grandfather "played the guitar beautifully; he serenaded this woman with his guitar." But their parents discouraged the union. After the lovers eloped, the parents disinherited their daughter and never spoke to her again.

Those were just a few of the stories passed down from the Castilla family. In short, though, we didn't come from the family's moneyed side.

So, I had a strong sense of my Spanish family tree and its colorful history going back generations. This was not the case on my father's side. I never met my father's father; he died while we were living in Spain due to complications of a stroke. I knew my African American grandmother but had no true understanding of the history of our ancestors. And my father did not talk much about his past.

When I moved to North Carolina to join Atrium Health, I got to thinking: *Here in Charlotte, I must not be very far from Charleston and the Cape Fear River where many Africans came ashore in slave ships.* But I just didn't know. And I had a desire to learn about my father's side. I had little knowledge of my father's kin—who they were, and where they came from—where *I* came from. It was like living in a big city where half of the town is well-lit and the other half is completely dark. I wanted to explore what existed in the dark that I couldn't see.

Marcus Garvey, the founder of the Universal Negro Improvement Association and the African Communities League, said, "A person without a sense of where he came from is like a tree without roots."

In many ways, I felt that. So, in 2018, I commissioned a DNA test and genealogy research into my family's past. The result, a report of fifty-plus pages, made it real. I am a descendent of slaves. The clue to the missing piece of my identity was written in script in the will of a slaveholder named Citizen Stovall Woods, living in Carroll County, Tennessee.

Slave schedules from the mid-1800s revealed that Woods owned eighteen African slaves, two of whom were called Grace and Ann. The references to Grace and Ann only by their first names in Woods's will indicated that they did not have surnames at the time, proof of their enslaved status prior to the adoption of the Thirteenth Amendment to the U.S. Constitution in 1865, which officially abolished slavery.

If Citizen Woods had not included "Grace and Ann" in his will, I might never have discovered my ancestors. A slave's existence was documented only if her owners created official records; slaves were considered chattel, items of property. That is why searching one's roots is so very difficult for Black Americans; the federal census only began recording African descendants in 1870. Grace and Ann appear in the 1870 census with the last name Woods, likely because in small, rural communities, like those in Carroll County, census takers often recorded former slaves with the surnames of their last owners. With their last names recorded, Grace and Ann became indelibly linked to the rest of my ancestors on my father's side. The pieces of the puzzle started falling into place.

This fascinating genealogy research revealed details my father never shared. I learned that my grandparents separated when my father was three. My grandmother was ultimately left to raise nine kids in rural Tennessee. She was a very strong-willed woman. My grandfather remarried and enlisted in the army, where he became an engineer, ultimately building bridges during World War II. I discovered through the documents that my grandfather never advanced past the fourth grade, which caused me to reflect on how very blessed I am. My father and mother didn't have the opportunity to go to college like I did. By the grace of God, I found my way through Penn State University and progressed into a successful career. And my sons Marcus and Antonio have benefited from higher education, too.

There's a widely used T-shirt slogan that's been attributed to African American visual artist and filmmaker Brandan Odums that you may have heard: "I am my ancestors' wildest dreams." I feel as if I am the result of those dreams.

Not all that long ago, my ancestors were working the fields as slaves and sharecroppers in North Carolina and Tennessee. Now I was leading one of the largest healthcare systems in the Southeast, responsible for the well-being of thousands of descendants of slaves and those who enslaved them.

My ancestors toiled day and night with the singular hope that a brighter day would come for their descendants. And, for me, seeing the actual birth, death, marriage, and property deeds of my ancestors made my responsibilities all the more real and present. I was able to live up to their hopes and dreams. I feel that today more than ever, because the opportunities for that American dream have dimmed for millions. Today it's so hard for so many people to realize that dream, without intentional work by organizations like Atrium Health and other organizations, to disrupt the root cause of systemic inequities. And helping them achieve it requires a three-legged stool of commitment from business, government, and community organizations. Collectively, more than ever, we need to create a system where the American dream can flourish again.

A Deed of Ownership

One evening, as I sat reading through my genealogy report, I came across a digital scan of the "Carroll County, TN, Register of Deeds, 1861." A green arrow added by the researchers pointed to a section of a deed of ownership written in the hand of a man named Yancy Bledsoe, who was originally from Wake County, North Carolina—about two and a half hours from where I was living in Charlotte. He had moved with his family and slaves to Tennessee; records indicated he was the largest slaveholder in Carroll County at the time. The court paper documented that on June 31, 1861, Bledsoe transferred ownership of a "girl Ann aged about eighteen and her child Stephen aged about two" to his sons, Jacob and William.

This Ann was not the Ann in the will of Citizen Woods, but Ann *Bledsoe*, mother of Stephen Hampton. They also were my direct ancestors, slaves gifted to Bledsoe's sons in the deed of ownership, as if they were cattle or plots of land—property. The genealogy report contained another detail, an annotation written in 1853 by abolitionist William Goodell. It summed up the prevailing attitudes of local Southern governments and plantation owners of the time: "The slave has no rights. . . The slave is not ranked among sentient beings, but among things."

I just sat there in my chair feeling numb for a few minutes and reread those words: "The slave is not ranked among sentient beings, but among things"—a piece of property without feelings.

I pulled out the ancestor chart from the genealogy report and followed my lineage from 1810 forward: Stephen Hampton, son of Ann Bledsoe, had a daughter named Irma Hampton. Irma married Agen Woods, the grandson of Grace (Gracie) Woods, the former slave who took care of Citizen Woods's wife after emancipation. Agen and Irma Woods were the parents of James Hobert Woods, my father's father, the grandfather I never knew.

My family tree illustrated to me how close I was to the days of slavery, only four generations. Even in their wildest dreams they could not have imagined that a descendant of theirs would one day be the CEO of one of the largest healthcare systems in the nation, one responsible for providing healing and hope to all, including the many descendants of African slaves in states in which most Africans arrived in ships from across the Atlantic.

Building on the Past

Researching my past was a deeply personal experience that I'm sharing because it is on the shoulders of those ancestors that I now stand. They forged a path through unwelcoming territory, to make the way a little easier for those who followed in their footsteps. I'm indebted to them and to others who helped break a path for me, like my mentor, Thomas D. Robinson.

About thirty years ago, fresh out of college, I was an enthusiastic, idealistic young professional with a vision to make a big difference in healthcare. I wanted to change the system, to protect innocent people like my Aunt Carmen, who suffered due to mistakes and mismanagement. I worked for Tom Robinson in my first healthcare job after graduate school, at Tyrone Hospital in Tyrone, Pennsylvania, where Tom was the chief executive officer. He saw something in me that I didn't even see in myself. He believed in me and gave me challenging assignments so that I could learn and grow. He unselfishly introduced me to a network of influential executives who helped guide my career.

A couple years later, when I was in the running for a CEO position at a hospital in Maryland, Tom graciously recommended me as a top candidate. After going through the interview process, the chair of the hospital's board of directors confided in Tom that while they considered me the most qualified candidate, Eastern Maryland, the same area where Frederick Douglass was born into slavery, wasn't quite ready for a Black man to run their hospital.

He did add that he wouldn't be surprised to see me someday in the pages of *Modern Healthcare*—which was the industry's leading hospital publication. On one hand, I wasn't surprised. At the time, fewer than 1 percent of hospital CEOs were African American. Tom was upset and told the board chairman that he was right—I *was* the best candidate for the position—and that one day the board would realize their mistake.[1]

Now, the thing about Tom is that he always focused on the bright spot of most any issue he dealt with, despite the discrimination he faced throughout his career. It's one of the lessons I picked up from him. After becoming one of the few Black graduates in his college class, he was hired as an accountant at a large tobacco firm, but he was denied company-sponsored housing because of the color of his skin. Tom had to live in a hotel for months before the company chauffeur invited him to live with his family. Eventually, Tom worked his way up through the ranks in his profession, earning the respect and admiration of many, both Black and white. He became the first Black member to serve on several important boards in his community. And with the support of his wife, Bonnie, Tom ultimately built a successful healthcare career, blazing a trail for countless African Americans to follow, including me.

Time to Move Mountains

Besides Tom Robinson and my family, I also owe a deep debt of gratitude to those healthcare pioneers who had a direct hand in helping Atrium Health become who we are today. I'm talking about the founders of Good Samaritan Hospital, the first hospital to serve the African American community of Charlotte. It had just twenty beds when it was established in 1891 with funds raised by St. Peter's Episcopal Church. The facility, nicknamed "Good Sam," grew substantially over the decades. Still, by the end of World War II, it was the only Charlotte-area hospital that would care for Black patients and employ Black doctors, who could not practice at any of the other hospitals in the region.

In the spring of 2020, I found myself at Bank of America Stadium, home to the Charlotte Panthers NFL football team, reading a historical marker that placed the former site of Good Samaritan Hospital at about the forty-yard line. That day, right there in the stadium were dozens of tables and tents bearing Atrium Health signage. The stadium was the location of what would end up being one of the nation's largest and most effectively managed mass vaccination sites.

I was there to observe the progress, find out if the teams needed anything, and engage with people as they waited for their shots. Our focus was not just to provide the lifesaving vaccine but to create the type of experience we would want our parents to have—which meant ensuring that patients did not have long waits. On day two, I noticed that the team had anticipated rain and erected a 100-yard-long covered walkway to the entrance.

Every detail mattered. I looked around the field that was filled with staff members from Atrium and our partner, Charlotte-based Honeywell. They were preparing for the more than 20,000 people who would enter the stadium during the three-day event, and I realized how far we'd come in helping the underserved and vulnerable since the days of Good Sam. Thirty percent of those we vaccinated were people of color, which was not the experience nationally. We worked with African American church groups to make sure their members had easy access to the schedule and to transportation. Our goal was to remove as many barriers as possible. But what also came to mind was how much farther we needed to go to create systemic, root-level changes as the pandemic illuminated the fundamental racial inequities in American society. COVID-19 dispro-portionately impacted people of color in devastating ways; in June 2020, the Centers for Disease Control and Prevention (CDC) reported that Black, Hispanic, American Indian, and Alaska Native people were twice as likely to die from COVID-19 as their white counterparts.[2]

The cold reality, however, was that none of this should have come as a shock or surprise. Since 1619, when the privateer White Lion was the first slave ship to arrive in Hampton, Virginia, a year before the *Mayflower* landed in Plymouth, Massachusetts, healthcare atrocities and disparities for African Americans have persisted.

In Harriet Washington's masterful 2007 book, *Medical Apartheid: The Dark History of Medical Experimentation on Black Americans from Colonial Times to the Present*, the bioethicist argues that "diverse forms of racial discrimination have shaped both the relationship between white physicians and black patients and the attitude of the latter towards mod-ern medicine in general."[3] Her book documents in chilling detail how both slaves and freedmen have been used as unwilling and unwitting experimental subjects by the medical establishment. It's certainly an eye-opener. Sure, I had read in college about the government's notorious Tuskegee Experiment. But I had no idea of the breadth of the shock-ing mistreatment and experimental exploitation until I read *Medical Apartheid*.

Two particular revelations stand out: After emancipation, Washington reports, Black people were unwittingly sterilized at very high rates. Why? The book explains that it was because their children were no longer valued after slavery was abolished.

And then there's the horrific story of medical malpractice by James Marion Sims, a surgeon who in the 1800s experimented on female slaves to find a cure for vesicovaginal fistulas. Incredibly, Sims did not give the women anesthesia before the painful surgeries, claiming the procedure was not painful enough to justify the trouble and citing the popular belief that Black people did not feel pain in the same way as white people—a belief that still permeates some circles today. Washington, a bioethicist and former fellow at Harvard Medical School, also detailed Sims's horrific experiments on infants—in one instance, he opened a Black baby's skull using a shoemaker's tools to prove his belief that Black infants' skulls grew faster than those of white babies, preventing proper cognitive development.

Washington's prodigious research into this previously unexplored history of abuse revealed for the first time the underlying roots of Black peoples' historic mistrust of research and the medical establishment. She calls the chasm in care it fostered "medical apartheid." In a 2007 interview with National Public Radio, when her book launched, Washington described medical apartheid as "the race-driven, very wide disparities in access to healthcare, quality of healthcare and protection of human rights" that still exists today. She told NPR's Farai Chideya, "All these racial disparities have led to such a wide gulf, a gulf that's really driven our nation to the point where, ten years ago, the health of Harlem men more closely resembles Bangladeshis' than their Manhattan neighbors. And this is the picture throughout the entire country. Black people are dying in droves of detectable, preventable, curable diseases."[4]

While Washington's exhaustive fact-finding shone a glaring spotlight on the medical atrocities of the past, it wasn't the first research to highlight the root cause of health disparities among African Americans. The earliest study on the health and welfare of Blacks was done in 1899. *The Philadelphia Negro* was commissioned by the University of Pennsylvania and published by sociologist and author W. E. B. Du Bois and a team of researchers.[5] With careful statistical analysis and survey data, the report meticulously chronicled the lives and lifestyles of middle-class, working-class, and unemployed Black Philadelphians and how they were affected by racial segregation in housing, economic opportunity, and access to healthy food and environments—the social determinants of health. The study demonstrated how these structured inequities manifested themselves as differences in health, illness, life, and death. Du Bois concluded that the health disparities highlighted in the report should "act as a spur for increased effort . . . and not as an excuse for passive indifference, or increased discrimination."[6]

In my author's note, I referenced the seminal study *Unequal Treatment: Confronting Racial and Ethnic Disparities in Healthcare*, which concluded essentially the same thing. After looking at 900 peer-reviewed papers that controlled for variables such as health insurance status, socioeconomic status, etc., those researchers found that race, stereotyping, and bias were the key factors in unequal care and outcomes. One of the members of the committee, David Williams, said, "I still remember one of the early meetings of the committee: when Jack Geiger presented his review of the literature there was a hush in the room. You could have heard a pin drop. The evidence was overwhelming that there was a problem."[7]

The 432-page tome is filled with study citations and statistics. Considered with the work of Du Bois and Washington, the data is more than determinative: racial inequities exist not just in wealth and economic mobility but most certainly in the life-and-death world of healthcare.

It is not a matter of gathering more data to prove the issue exists. The sad reality is that the gap in life expectancy among people of color has persisted with little progress. In fact, a 2023 study in the *Journal of the American Medical Association*, titled "Excess Mortality and Years of Potential Life Lost Among the Black Population in the US, 1990–2020," found that our nation's Black population experienced 1.63 million excess deaths and a loss of 80 million years of life.[8] Eighty million years of life! So, by every measure, we have enough data to unequivocally show that there are deep disparities.

What is required are not more studies, but action. What is required is not complacency when the media moves on to another breaking story, but an unwavering battle against indifference. What is required is not more feel-good talk, but a comprehensive and systemic approach that disrupts the root causes of inequities. Your zip code and color of your skin should not have a high correlation coefficient to your health. Not in this country.

As for systemic root causes, it means we must address in a comprehensive manner what are called the six social determinants of health: nutrition, physical environment, community, healthcare access, financial stability, and education. In fact, 80 to 90 percent of health outcomes—including chronic diseases like diabetes and heart disease—emerge from those factors, with poverty being one of the most impactful, according to the American Academy of Family Physicians.[9] The *Journal of the American Medical Association* found that the gap in life expectancy between the richest 1 percent and poorest 1 percent of individuals was 14.6 years for men and 10.1 years for women.[10] In other words, health is not just about what happens within hospital walls.

That's just one point of reference among many. Consider some of these 2020 statistics from the Center for American Progress[11] and the CDC:

- Thirteen percent of Black Americans and 10 percent of Latinx report having fair or poor health, compared with 8 percent of non-Hispanic whites.
- Black Americans have the highest mortality rate for all cancers, compared with any other racial and ethnic group.
- Twenty-one percent of Hispanic adults have been diagnosed with diabetes, compared with 13 percent of white adults.
- Asian Americans are 40 percent more likely to be diagnosed with diabetes than non-Hispanic white Americans.

These are sobering numbers, for sure—but they can be changed.

Here is one example of how we're addressing racial and ethnic disparities, a success story of which I'm very proud: in recent years, Atrium Health's information systems team redesigned our EMR, our electronic medical record system, transforming the way we collect demographic data. We revamped our questions on race, ethnicity, language preference, assigned sex at birth, gender identity, and location, and we created a tool that organizes all that data for population health and clinical quality measures like diabetes, blood sugar control, blood pressure monitoring, cancer screenings, readmissions, and more. Analyzing this depth of data for trends and insights, we were able to take action. We implemented a number of culturally appropriate interventions at primary care practices. We worked with community partners on a phone call campaign and collaborated with a Spanish-language newspaper to publicize the risk of colorectal cancer in the Hispanic population. We announced free screening opportunities at local events, and the impact was huge, resulting in an additional focused screening, which helped us find cancers at early stages. From 2018 to 2019, Atrium Health closed the disparity of colorectal screenings for Hispanic males by 62.7 percent. The Centers for Medicare & Medicaid Services (CMS) acknowledged that effort by choosing Atrium for its prestigious CMS Heath Equity Award, the only nonprofit health system in the nation to be so recognized.

We also closed the gap between people of color and the white population in COVID-19 deaths in our region, thanks to the lifesaving vaccines and our mass vaccination efforts, like those held at the football stadium and Charlotte Motor Speedway, where we had shots going into arms at a rate of one every 4.5 seconds. Those are big steps forward. But as I said in June 2020, "There's not a vaccine for racism."[12]

Decades after the Civil Rights Act of 1964 ended legal segregation, de facto segregation in schools, housing, and employment persists, allowing economic inequality to endure. President Lyndon Johnson signed this most sweeping civil rights legislation since Reconstruction into law on July 2, 1964—seven days before I was born—after addressing the nation with these words: "My fellow citizens, we have come now to a time of testing. We must not fail. Let us close the springs of racial poison. . . . Let us lay aside irrelevant differences and make our nation whole."[13] And yet, nearly sixty years later, our nation is divided still. Toxic notions once on the fringes of society have infiltrated the mainstream American political and cultural landscape. Antisemitism, hate crimes against Asian Americans, and fear of immigrants are on the rise. And entrenched patterns of discrimination continue to systematically exclude minorities and people of color from opportunities and the American dream.

From my tenure as chairman of the Federal Reserve Bank of Richmond, I saw firsthand research highlighting firsthand the gaps and the depth of inequality in our nation. African Americans have only ten cents in wealth for every dollar that white Americans own. Since wealth can be passed down from one generation to another, this gap reveals intergenerational impacts of the systemic racism of the past. The roadblocks that previous generations faced, through practices like redlining and lack of access to the GI Bill among Black troops returning home from World War II, continue to affect their children and grandchildren.

And from the data, we know unequivocally that people with greater income and wealth simply live longer and healthier lives. They can afford health insurance, which provides access to preventative and wellness care. But healthcare access is only the tip of the iceberg. They can also afford to live in safer neighborhoods, with better schools and parks and places to exercise. They can afford access to transportation, healthy food options, and in many cases hospitals and healthcare providers. We need to recognize that the disparities in health are inextricably linked to disparities in income and wealth, and we can't begin to solve the former unless we commit to also solving the latter.

As a man of color, I feel personally responsible for being part of the solution. I owe that to the shoulders I stand on, all those who've helped me along the path—people like my board chair Edward J. Brown III, who passed away in April 2023 after a valiant battle with cancer. Ed ran Hendrick Motors as CEO for over a decade and before that spent thirty-two years as Hugh McColl's chief lieutenant, helping him build Bank of America. Hugh told me multiple times that Ed was his go-to person to deal with the most complex challenges at the bank. Ed was perfectly suited to help guide our board during the most transformative times in our history—growing from a regional to national system. As brilliant as Ed was at business, he had an even bigger heart and was all in on matters of diversity and equity. His passion shone through and infused every part of our organization. And he was anti-status-quo on anything. Early in my tenure, he gave me a stamp to keep at my desk, with a big, red X over the phrase, "The way we have always done it." I have said often that an organization can only go as far as a board can see or as fast as the management team can move. Ed helped Atrium Health go both far and fast in just about every strategic initiative we had—most of which was the commitment to moving the dial on health equity.

A Model for Equity

In 2016, we established a new mission statement for Atrium Health: "To improve Health, elevate Hope, and advance Healing—for all." It reflected the fact that people came to us for health and healing, for sure, but they also came to us for hope. When a mother brings her sick child into one of our emergency rooms, she is coming to us for all three—health, hope, and healing. And healing is not only physical but emotional.

Most important was the *FOR ALL* part. It was intentionally broad, encompassing much more than clinical healthcare, because we know that health starts in our homes, in our kitchens, our schools, workplaces, neighborhoods, and communities. So, Atrium Health embarked on ambitious equity initiatives inside and outside our hospital walls. Our goal was to chart a new path forward for how hospital systems, businesses, community organizations, and government entities can partner together to defeat injustice and close health and life expectancy gaps. To formulate new coalitions and approaches.

Improving the health of our most vulnerable communities is not just about providing more cancer screenings and health clinics in low-income neighborhoods. It's about raising the standard of living for the residents in those neighborhoods. And the one proven thing that families need in order to establish the kind of self-sufficiency they need for upward mobility is stable and affordable housing.

A study by researchers at Stanford University's Center on Poverty and Inequality in 2015 analyzed intergenerational wealth and economic mobility in fifty U.S. cities. The upshot of the report: a child growing up in poverty in many of those urban cities has little chance of growing out of poverty as an adult. "In the lowest-mobility areas of the United States, which tend to be in the south," the researchers concluded, "fewer than 1 in 20 poor children reach the top quintile (in income when they are adults), a rate that is lower than in any developed country for which data have been analyzed to date." Charlotte was ranked last, a wake-up call that helped to galvanize the entire community and sparked a movement to become a model city for inclusive opportunity.

And we as a health system committed to being part of the solution, by addressing food insecurity and housing. In fact, in 2019, we committed $10 million to help fund affordable housing initiatives in Charlotte. We joined Truist Financial Corporation, along with several other companies, foundations, and individuals, as investors in the $58 million Housing Impact Fund (HIF), which purchases complexes on the private market known as "naturally occurring affordable housing," or NOAHs.

The NOAH approach is a fast and effective method for addressing housing insecurity, by preserving low-rent structures. HIF purchases housing that would otherwise fall into disrepair or be snapped up by redevelopers turning them into high-rent luxury apartments. HIF preserves low-rent structures that still provide investors with a modest return. HIF units average $728 per month, which is half the cost of average apartment rent in Charlotte. The majority of the households currently in the program earn between 30 and 60 percent of the area median income (AMI), and 30 percent of the units housing those residents offer rents of $300 monthly or less. What's more, most of these apartment complexes are near areas of economic opportunity.

The HIF/NOAH program is simply good business, with a profound social impact. It also gave us an opportunity to help our own employees through our HOPE housing assistance initiative. HOPE, which stands for Housing Opportunity Promoting Equity, provides Atrium Health teammates facing hardships and earning a household income between $16,600 and $63,300 with NOAH housing opportunities.

Atrium Health's investment in housing is in addition to the $2 billion our health system invests each year—more than $5.7 million every day— in uncompensated care and other community benefits as the state's largest safety net provider. To address hunger, through collaborative community engagement programs, we've established a Kids Eat Free program, which provides healthy, nutritious meals to thousands of children each summer, and, in partnership with Loaves & Fishes, piloted the first-ever food pharmacy in our community that gives patients access to healthy food options. We also invested into our Caregiver Heroes Teammate Emergency Care Fund, which awards payouts of up to $10,000 to staff involved in direct patient care who've struggled physically, emotionally, and financially during the pandemic.

One of Atrium Health's greatest milestones that builds upon all these initiatives was breaking ground on the second campus of Wake Forest University School of Medicine in 2022. Charlotte's first four-year medical school will extend Atrium Health's (now Advocate Health's) ability to provide equity in both access to healthcare and education. As the largest educator of physicians and other medical professionals in North Carolina, Atrium Health had been educating nearly 3,200 total learners across more than 100 specialized programs each year. But through pipeline partnerships, between Charlotte's historically Black college Johnson C. Smith University, Carolinas College of Health Sciences, Cabarrus College of Health Sciences, and the new Wake Forest University School of Medicine campus in Charlotte, even more students from disadvantaged and low-income communities will have equal opportunity to pursue careers in health sciences. Those initiatives include our $10 million Bishop George E. Battle Jr. Scholarship Endowment to support health sciences education for those who live in underserved communities. The endowment honors Bishop Battle, an emeritus member of the Atrium Health Board of Commissioners and the Atrium Health Foundation Board and a lifelong advocate for North Carolina's at-risk and economically disadvantaged communities.

These efforts are critically important not only for our region but for our nation, because while the minority population has ballooned over the past forty years, the overall number of minority physicians is dismally low. Among active physicians, only 6 percent identify as African American, according to the American Association of Medical Colleges. And African Americans represent 13 percent of the population of this country. This disparity is alarming on a number of levels, including its potential impact on health outcomes. Research suggests quite strongly that people of color need far greater access to culturally connected physicians who understand their lives, lifestyles, and challenges as much as their clinical needs. In 2018, a study by Stanford University's Institute for Economic Policy Research looked at the effect of diversity in the physician workforce of Oakland, California, on preventive care among African American men. The researchers randomized Black patients to

Black or non-Black male medical doctors and found that participants were more likely to accept preventive measures, particularly invasive procedures, after meeting with a Black doctor. Specifically looking at cardiovascular health, the researchers concluded that Black doctors could reduce the Black-white male gap in mortality by 19 percent.[14]

Our goal is for the two medical school campuses in Winston-Salem and Charlotte to begin to bridge that gap, by producing one of the most diverse health sciences institutions in the country, turning out generations of medical professionals who are representative of the communities they will serve. In the next decade, we intend for the Wake Forest University School of Medicine expansion to create a preeminent regional corridor for health technology, medical education, research, and innovation that will bring new medicines and treatments to patients while advancing economic equity in the region.

Our vision is intentionally audacious. There are mountains to move. But our feeling is, if not us, then who? I'm encouraged because of something that my mentor Tom Robinson shared with me long ago, a single motivational line: "You have been assigned this mountain to show others it can be moved."

The discrimination Tom faced in his career—the mountains he had to move—were all for others who would come behind him. People like me.

I remember how Tom liked to recite the lyrics to a gospel song by Rev. F. C. Barnes, of Rocky Mount, North Carolina, called "Rough Side of the Mountain." "I am climbing up the rough side of the mountain just trying to make it home," he'd sing. Because Tom showed me that he could move his own mountains, and because many before me moved theirs to make my climb up the rough side a little smoother, I know that it's my turn and that of the colleagues I am fortunate to work with daily, a phenomenal team that shares the same passion.

When we understand where we come from, we can better understand—and appreciate—our place in the world.

"Grace and Ann Woods, property of Citizen S. Woods."
"A girl Ann aged about eighteen and her child Stephen,
bequeathed by Yancy Bledsoe to his sons."

Knowing the names of my slave ancestors helps me to wake up each day with a greater sense of gratitude, purpose, and energy. We all are beneficiaries of the struggles and hopes of our people who came before us. And we have a responsibility to pay that forward.

CHAPTER 6

Not Enuff Joy

Injustice anywhere is a threat to justice everywhere. We are caught in an inescapable network of mutuality, tied in a single garment of destiny. Whatever affects one directly, affects all indirectly.

Letter from a Birmingham Jail
Martin Luther King Jr.
16 April 1963

On May 25, 2020, with the country already emotionally drained from COVID-19, the ground shifted for all of us once more as we witnessed the brutal killing of George Floyd, recorded on cell phone video. It was hard to watch Minneapolis police officer Derek Chauvin pressing his knee on the neck of Floyd—a man described by his brother Roger as a gentle giant who would never hurt anybody—for eight minutes and fifteen seconds. Later we learned that Chauvin's knee remained against Floyd's airway even after he lost consciousness and for a full minute and twenty seconds after paramedics arrived.

That night, I found myself wide awake, staring at the clock . . . 12:24 a.m., 2:12 a.m., 3:51 a.m. . . . as I tossed and turned. I couldn't shake the images from my mind. It very well could have been one of my uncles who found themselves in an unfortunate moment of fate. Or one of my friends. Or me.

The next day, I met with Fernando Little, who was Atrium Health's chief diversity officer, and others from across our system. Everyone was numb; it was as if a member of our own family had been killed. The repeated imagery of Floyd's murder on social media and news reports recounting past shooting deaths of Black people reopened the deep wounds: Tamir Rice, Stephon Clark, Breonna Taylor—all dead for what had been minor infractions. Case in point was Eric Garner, who was being arrested for selling single cigarettes from packs without tax stamps when a police officer put him in a prohibited chokehold; a medical examiner ruled his death a homicide. And then there was unarmed twenty-five-year-old Ahmaud Arbery, murdered in a hate crime by white men while he was jogging through a Georgia neighborhood. The domino effect of these senseless tragedies was stirring something in the nation's core; you could feel it: a tipping point. Countless years of intolerance and injustice boiled over in eight minutes and fifteen seconds and spurred nationwide protests. Fernando told me he felt that Floyd's death would deeply affect Atrium Health teammates in the coming days and weeks—and the teams would want to hear from me directly. The tragedy rekindled my own painful recollections of the racial discrimination I'd experienced throughout my life as the offspring of an interracial couple.

My father, Eugene, was African American; my mother, Maria, is Spanish. "Miscegenation" was still illegal in many states when they married in 1963, so they wed in Spain. Interracial marriage wasn't fully legal in all U.S. states until 1967, three years after I was born, when the Supreme Court decision, *Loving v. Virginia*, decreed all state anti-miscegenation laws unconstitutional.

As a small child, we would travel south to visit my grandmother on my dad's side in rural Tennessee. My father would have my mother ride in the back seat of the car with us kids as we drove through town, lest we get pulled over and be questioned about why a white woman would be sitting next to a Black driver, our dad, in the front seat. And my mother would have a blanket in the back seat just in case, to cover us if we were pulled over so we could pretend to be sleeping.

When we would visit my grandmother in Tennessee, Dad also refused to allow my mother to take us shopping without his sisters, for fear of what people might do if they saw a white woman alone with two "colored" children.

I never really shared those memories at work. If anything, like many people of color, I tried to keep my personal experience with respect to race out of the workplace as I rose to become one of the few African American executives working in hospital administration. I knew I had to earn my successes through sheer determination and performance. Any discussions of race and its impact on me and my family always seemed to be a minefield-laden road, because race has never been something the country is comfortable speaking about—and I knew it could have unpredictable consequences on how it impacted me in my career and ultimately my ability to put food on the table for my family. So, I kept it to myself.

After the nationwide social justice protests and renewed calls for racial equality in the wake of George Floyd's killing, Kinneil Coltman, who oversaw our social impact division, asked me a simple question: "Are you willing to be vulnerable enough to truly share your experiences with racism?" She added that she believed by doing so I would help create a safe space for others as well, others who might mistakenly assume that since I was the CEO I had somehow been immune to prejudice.

Her question led me to reflect upon something I read in Stephen M. R. Covey's book *The Speed of Trust*—that integrity is about conforming reality to our words. And if leadership is about establishing high-trust relationships, I knew I had to speak my truth—to model creating a safe space, to be vulnerable enough to share one's own personal struggles, with hope that they can be overcome. So, for the first time in my career, I found myself sharing openly the stories of my past as a Black man in this country.

The first thing I did in the days following the Floyd tragedy was write this letter, abridged here, to our employees:

> Like so many of you who have reached out to me directly, I have battled with some very deep emotions many times over this past week as I reflected upon the senseless death of George Floyd on the streets of Minneapolis. I am heartbroken and distressed after watching another use of excessive force that ended a life prematurely.

We should be better than this as a country. We must be better than this.

Personally, it has evoked painful memories from discriminatory events that I have experienced as a person of color. And it is why I selected healthcare as a career—to help create solutions that reduce health disparities and structural injustice.

I am reminded of when Dr. Martin Luther King Jr. was jailed in Birmingham, Alabama, for peacefully protesting the inequality taking place nearly 50 years ago. While there, he wrote:

"Injustice anywhere is a threat to justice everywhere. We are caught in an inescapable network of mutuality, tied in a single garment of destiny. Whatever affects one directly, affects all indirectly."

These powerful words ring as true today as they did decades ago. It is clear that so many across our system are hurting—and not just our teammates of color, but teammates from all walks of life who feel outraged and want to work together peacefully to create a better world.

Let this be the defining moment in which we collectively embrace the humanity we share and banish the hatred and attitudes that have led to acts of racial intolerance. I truly believe that the strength of our collective voice as Atrium Health in standing against injustice is more powerful than any evil that exists.

Courageous Conversations

My father also didn't like to talk about racism he had faced, but he did share one story he experienced in the navy when he first joined and met his new bunkmate, a white man from Arkansas. My father always had this gregarious way about him, and he had an internal sense of confidence. His roommate, although a big fella, seemed painfully shy and quiet around my dad. He would avert his eyes whenever Dad attempted to engage him in conversation. My father, six foot three himself and imposing in his own right, knowing that they would be spending months together in quarters only slightly bigger than a bathroom, was trying to find some sort of bridge with this guy who rarely spoke. Then one night, my father heard sobbing coming from the bottom bunk. This eighteen-year-old kid was crying, so Dad jumped down.

"Hey, man, what's the trouble?" he asked.

After a few minutes of Dad's inquiry, the man came clean: "My daddy don't like me bunking with no nigger . . . and I can't say as I'm happy about it either."

Dad's reaction? He laughed. "Well, my friend, welcome to the navy. You're gonna have to stop worrying about what your daddy thinks. If you can do that, you'll be all right. Now, shut up so I can get some sleep."

My father could disarm anyone with his laughter and his charm. It just took a little extra time in this case, but eventually he got through to his bunkmate—not as people of different colors, but man to man. They were men bound by the shared desire to serve this great nation and earn a living for their families. And they fast became friends. In fact, during Christmas leave, Dad's bunkmate went home to visit his folks in Arkansas and confronted his family. "You raised me completely wrong about colored folks," he told them. "Eugene is a good man; he's my friend." That all happened just six years after President Harry S. Truman issued an executive order on July 26, 1948, banning segregation in the armed forces. Were it not for that, they would have been in separate bunks, and the opportunity for breaking down a barrier and making a new friend would have never occurred.

I share that story because it speaks volumes about how these beliefs are embedded and passed along, many times not even questioned by later generations. But it also offers hope in the power of connecting at a human level, of laughing together, of breaking bread together. But also, if we truly want to comprehend the roots of anger and despair that have gripped our Black and Brown fellow neighbors and citizens, then we need to have deep and real conversations about the generational challenges being faced. We have to fundamentally shake up the status quo. Those conversations must be intentional and honest, like my father's was with his bunkmate. And they must be spoken in a safe space, where Black and white people can openly share thoughts, feelings, and ideas without judgment and in a respectful, solution-oriented way.

Within weeks of the George Floyd murder, Fernando Little, who was leading our office of diversity and inclusion, dramatically scaled a program called "Courageous Conversations," to provide an opportunity for dialogue and healing, allowing teams to examine their personal reactions to both the trauma in Minneapolis and related historic racial issues within our own community. It began with a system-wide, three-part virtual series allowing our diverse men's and women's system resource groups to share their personal stories, perspectives, and emotions, in a safe space, to begin the healing process. Next, the office of diversity and inclusion hosted more than 300 hours of small group programming, open to all teammates, which resulted in over 13,000 teammate interactions. Fernando and his team also developed a Racial Justice Toolkit of readings, videos, call-to-action strategies, a Twenty-One-Day Racism Awareness Challenge, and a facilitator's guide with discussion prompts to help initiate these Courageous Conversations. Here's a sample of some of those questions that the guide encourages each one of us to ask ourselves.

1. How are you personally affected by the recent events/shootings?
2. How does what happened in Ferguson, Baltimore, New York, Charleston, Tulsa, Charlotte, Minneapolis, and other locations impact your feelings of physical and/or mental comfort/security or safety?
3. From your perspective, are race and/or racism at play in this story?
4. Can the climate and what is happening in our larger communities have an impact on how we deal with patients and families? If so, how?
5. What must we confront that's "in the ground" in our community and in ourselves in order to interrupt the culture of fear and violence toward "the other"?
6. Can you share some strategies you have used that have confronted and interrupted the culture of fear and/or violence?
7. What can you commit to do as an individual, to be a part of a solution?

We also provided training sessions for leaders to engage with their teams. Diversity and Inclusion held a series of leader-only education programs about racial justice, to help leaders support teammates through the emotion curve, by connecting and initiating conversations, mitigating unconscious bias, and working through scenarios and best practices for leading during these unprecedented times. One of our white leaders said in one of the sessions, "I thought I was fairly 'woke' until I had a conversation with my daughter over dinner, who educated me about discrimination her close college friends of color had experienced."

A word about the word "woke." The word is now being used as culture war fodder in ways that obfuscates its intended meaning. The Merriam-Webster dictionary defines it as "aware of and actively attentive to important societal facts and issues (especially issues of racial and social justice)."[1] If inequities irrefutably exist, then what is wrong with actively being attentive to them? With being awake? Going back to my father's service in the military, there was a saying I heard often: "Stay frosty." I always took it to mean to stay alert and vigilant. To me, there are similarities with the word "woke," which was first used by African Americans in the 1940s, to mean "stay awake and vigilant (frosty) to issues of injustice." That, in fact, was the reasoning behind our Courage Conversations initiative after the murder of George Floyd.

As a result of these programs, we witnessed beautiful acts of solidarity and our organizational culture grew even stronger. For example, in conjunction with the White Coats for Black Lives national movement, at many of our hospitals, physicians and other teammates took a knee to demonstrate support for eliminating racial bias in the practice of medicine.

Many of our teammates shared with us that in these programs they found comfort, support, and hope within their Atrium Health family. I heard about one of our teammates, who was so distraught and anxious following Floyd's death, she called out sick three days in a row. But after participating in our Courageous Conversations, she told us, "I felt proud, validated, and heard; it gave me the energy to keep going."

I took part in a number of these Courageous Conversations meetings with teammates and found them to be cathartic as well. In fact, within a couple weeks of George Floyd's death, I met with our Men's Diversity

Leadership Network, a group largely comprised of men of color from across our large enterprise. The group shared stories of injustice and how racism has impacted their lives. It was a painfully authentic conversation. One physician living in an affluent neighborhood said that he wouldn't let his sixteen-year-old son go jogging by himself at night, for fear of being harassed or worse. Another shared a story about being pulled over for his tire touching the white line while driving, and it turning out to be a full-hour narcotics search. This was someone who didn't even drink alcohol and was seen as a leader who built bridges in his community between the police and the neighborhood. In a way, it was cathartic to have a safe space to share all of this and to release some of the burdens and fears people bring into the workplace every single day. And for the first time in a work situation, I shared my own interactions with racism from growing up in the Philadelphia area and during my college years, being pulled over and searched for no reason, and being denied a prestigious fellowship because of what I looked like.

As each man shared his stories, other instances of discrimination bubbled up from the depths of my memory. For me, the meeting was a powerfully emotional moment that helped me realize the importance of sharing my story, when appropriate, to create the space for others to share their own—whether Black, LGBTQ, Asian, Latino, etc. I realized that it was a key part of my responsibilities—to promote spaces where courageous conversations can happen. Through that experience, I came to recognize a new paradigm for leadership that my good friend and coach Nicholas Janni wrote a book about in 2022 (and which I wrote the foreword to), titled *Leader as Healer*. A key responsibility of leadership is to help heal . . . and that work starts from within. Listening, sharing, and healing is my fundamental calling and responsibility. And as Nicholas states, "*Leader as Healer* is in essence an urgent call to repair, to correct frameworks of thinking and acting in which doing eclipses being, and hyper-rational, analytical thinking relegates feeling, sensing, intuiting and the transpersonal to the outer fringes of life."[2]

This experience helped to affirm the importance of bringing my whole self to work, including my music, which has brought tremendous healing to my own life.

Not Enuff Joy

As I've mentioned before, I've played the electric guitar most of my life—rock, blues, jazz, you name it. When I was eleven, my parents bought me a Fender Stratocaster copycat guitar and amp for Christmas, skipping three months of rent payments to afford it. (Dad's pride kept him from asking the landlord for an extension to pay the rent; he made my mother do it!) After a few years of practice, I had blisters on my fingers, driving the neighbors nuts with Jimi Hendrix guitar riffs and playing in garage bands with friends in Warminster, Pennsylvania.

By the time I got to college, I played well enough that I used gigs with a classic rock-type band called Stolyn Hours to pay my tuition and living expenses at Penn State University. We were the most popular band in State College at the time, and I was earning $400, $500, even $1,000 on graduation weekend. Then, as a graduate student, I formed a ten-piece rhythm and blues band called Soul Gypsies that had promise. And I wrote a lot of songs. It was my form of expression, my own personal diary of sorts.

Ultimately, I came to a crossroads. We were offered a contract to do a mini tour at the same time I was offered a promotion to move to Virginia. I decided to take the promotion and a career in healthcare over music. But I never stopped writing music and playing guitar. In recent years, on rare occasions, I've brought my guitar out for public events like Atrium Health's annual staff talent show and the Dancing with the Stars of Charlotte Gala, benefiting local charities. It got me back in the groove and, in 2018, I picked it back up and once again started playing some of those old songs. With my passion for music rekindled, I found that having a creative outlet was a balm to my soul, and I ended up putting together some demos with a friend who, I learned, had recorded many of his own albums—as a songwriter, arranger, and producer. One thing led to another, and I decided to record an album of songs I had written over thirty-five years prior, working with a great, professional studio just fifteen minutes from my house. We even ended up putting together a band of incredibly talented musicians to play on this project, including Aaron Sterling, who has toured with John Mayer; Tyrone Jefferson, who ran James Brown's band for a decade; and Adrian Crutchfield, who was Prince's go-to saxophone player.

The day before a worldwide pandemic was declared, we recorded the rhythm tracks for eight of the songs, not knowing when and if we would ever be returning to complete the album. After George Floyd's murder and the protests for social justice and racial equality, those old tunes we had just recorded that I wrote in college started to take on a new purpose for me. Two of them in particular, "Walk in My Footsteps" and "Not Enuff Joy," written in my mid-twenties, are a window into how I was seeing my world at that age. The lyrics of the former, "Don't judge me until you walk in my footsteps," were written in response to what I saw every night on TV as a teen in the Philadelphia area— kids that looked like me being constantly intimidated, harassed, and arrested nightly, under the notoriously racist mayor of Philly at the time, Frank Rizzo—who once told supporters to "vote white."

And "Not Enuff Joy" was inspired by a documentary I had seen about war in Africa. It made me think about how, fundamentally, whether you're in Africa or Pennsylvania or anywhere, there's a common human element that we need to recognize. I wrote:

> When one brother is in chains, we should ALL feel the iron
> When one sister burns with pain, we should ALL feel the fire
> When is it ever gonna stop . . .
> I look around the world feeling so much shame
> Not enuff joy, too much pain, not enuff joy, too much pain.

I intended the song not as a protest but to send the message to never give up hope. I wanted to tell people of color in Africa and Philadelphia that, despite the cold realities they were living, there was good in the world. And I wanted to say that my greatest hope was that someday they could find a little joy.

In revisiting "Not Enuff Joy," I recognized that its message was very appropriate to the current time. And I had a forum in which to share it— Atrium Health's annual talent show. Due to COVID-19, it wouldn't be in-person and would be entirely prerecorded, so it made sense to develop the song into a music video. We shot the video at night in locations around Charlotte, including in front of a Black Lives Matter mural and on top of a parking garage. I wore a fedora and sunglasses, a nod to my grandfather, who wore a fedora, and to my father, who influenced me with his love for blues music. We filmed a flamenco dancer, to celebrate my mother's roots in Andalusia, Spain, the birthplace of flamenco dance. We even coaxed Charlotte Mayor Vi Lyles to make a cameo. In the middle of the exhaustion of battling the pandemic, it gave everyone a little reprieve and a reason to have a little fun.

Our Atrium Health talent show producers put the music video into the broadcast, which took place at the end of August 2020. It landed on YouTube in September. And now every employee in our hospital system knows my "secret" passion for playing guitar. People close to me know that I typically kept my music side separate from professional circles, but in the same spirit of sharing my own experiences as a biracial man, I got comfortable with having these worlds intersect, because the message I wrote as a young man is still relevant today, and it was fundamentally the same mission statement we had crafted when I first joined Atrium Health . . . to improve Health, elevate Hope, and advance Healing—*FOR ALL*.

Eventually, I completed my album, which was released in May 2022, called *Love and Protest*. Floyd's murder inspired me to write a new song called "Say My Name."

Say My Name

In the beginning
You didn't care to know my name
Invisible and silent
Just trying to make it through the day

But in one nine-minute moment
My world came to an end
But when this day is over
You will remember who I've been

Say my name (my name, my name . . .)

I danced with Nefertiti
Got my eagle at Corcoran

Started a Renaissance in Harlem
Wore a sign that "I'm a man"

Say my name . . .

Returned to soil and dust
Breath flowing like the wind
My soul forever rising
My light no longer dimmed

In one nine-minute moment
My world came to an end
But when this day is over
Won't ever kneel on me again

Say my name . . .

Health Equity and Social Impact

Lyrics can be inspiring, but without follow-up—without action—they
are just words. However, words put into action have the power to change
the world. And what we need right now is action. Inclusion and equity
efforts only have impact when you build them into your operating structures and make them a core part of your day-to-day business.

Atrium Health realized many years ago that addressing equity starts
from within. We must begin with ourselves. We've been intentional
about recruiting, retaining, and empowering a diverse workforce that is
representative of the communities we serve. For example, our office of
diversity and inclusion developed a diversity infrastructure made up of
nine system resource groups (SRGs) and ten diversity councils, tasked
with advancing the interests of patients and teammates, and we invite all
teammates to join one. These groups are not only resources for members,
but they have the power to transform our culture, to challenge the status
quo, and to urge us to do better.

To illustrate how we're challenging the status quo at Atrium Health,
I must brag a bit about our beloved board chair, Edward J. Brown III,
whom I previously mentioned. As the dual pandemics of COVID-19 and

racial injustice descended upon the nation, beginning in 2020, Ed recognized our chance to choose between community and chaos. He urged us to use the chaos of the year as a catalyst to completely reexamine how we can achieve greater social impact and eliminate the inequities we see. He challenged us to become a model for the nation's healthcare systems. Ed was our biggest champion for creating a social impact special committee of the board, to reengineer our Atrium Health Social Impact Strategy and make it the centerpiece of our entire corporate strategy. This social impact strategy is built on four main pillars, which are detailed below. You'll see these pillars threaded throughout our enterprise work as part of our new chapter as Advocate Health in later chapters as well.

Pillar 1: Equity in Access

To ensure equitable access to care across our geographic footprint, we must meet community members where they live, work, play, and worship. This means being intentional about where we build and operate our clinics, in zip codes that have historically experienced underinvestment and had fewer resources and less access to opportunity. And it also means taking healthcare beyond our physical walls, by expanding virtual visits for primary and specialty care, such as behavioral health and dieticians, and creating new, innovative ways to deliver care. For instance, during the pandemic we used our mobile units to test thousands of community members and partnered with fifty-five community sites, including organizations that disproportionately serve communities of color. These mobile testing units allowed us to close the testing disparity gap for Black and Hispanic populations.

Pillar 2: Equity in Quality and Outcomes

Our communities are broad and diverse. Across the Southeast, we serve dozens of ethnic communities and over seventy languages, which can present significant complexities, as not all patients can—or should—be treated the exact same way. Each has their own unique background and requires tailored, personal care. And the best way to do this is to draw on data. At Atrium Health, we rewired how we collect demographic data and used our Demographic Data Wall tool to identify clinical outcomes across populations and intervene to eliminate health disparities. We discovered a gap in colorectal cancer screening among Hispanic males in our data, for example, and were able to target and increase colorectal cancer screenings for this population.

Pillar 3: Equity in Acute Social Needs

While access to quality healthcare is often equated with good health, only 20 percent of health outcomes are tied to seeing a doctor or going to a clinic or hospital. Other factors, such as housing, education, employment, income, wealth, and the environment where we live and work, can determine our success, our health, and our life span. These factors are called "social determinants of health," or SDOH, and they represent the socioeconomic conditions of one's life, which has been shown to impact health outcomes by as much as 80 percent. At Atrium Health, we developed a standardized set of social determinants of health questions to ask all patients, to then be able to connect them to the resources they need, made possible through partnerships with community organizations.

People living at or near the poverty level often face many social challenges. They don't have access to and/or can't afford healthy food. They encounter issues such as evictions or challenges in paying for medications. They lack convenient, affordable transportation to healthcare. They don't have safe parks and green spaces for recreation. All of these challenges can affect one's health and well-being. At Atrium Health, we have worked to consistently screen our patients for these kinds of social needs, and we partner with community organizations that are meeting these immediate needs with efforts like placing mobile food pantries in low-income communities and sponsoring summer nutrition programs to provide free, nutritious meals for our children across North Carolina.

Pillar 4: Equity in Social Determinants of Health

While we know that we have a vital responsibility to connect our patients to social services and community-based organizations that can help address their needs—such as housing, food, transportation, and other factors—we also understand that we must work alongside partners at a local, regional, and national level to shore up the social safety net that affects health.

We do this work by studying the communities we serve, understanding where there are gaps, and then working to fill them through innovative solutions, such as investing in naturally occurring affordable housing or setting up a feeding program in our hospital cafeterias, for kids who don't have access to free lunches at school during the summer months.

We also work toward aligning with community organizations to advocate for legislative change, to support equity across all SDOHs. For example, Atrium Health partnered with the Federal Reserve Bank of Richmond and the Federal Reserve Bank of Atlanta, along with our local Goodwill and other workforce agencies and nonprofits, to develop the Benefits Cliff Community Lab. Benefits cliffs occur when getting a raise at work puts an employee above the income eligibility threshold for public assistance, such as childcare and housing programs, resulting in less overall household income at the end of the month. Launched in April 2023, the Benefits Cliff Community Lab provides access to the Career Ladder Identifier and Financial Forecaster (CLIFF), which helps employees and employers better understand the potential short- and long-term impact of benefit cliffs. The Benefits Cliff Community Lab also offers strategies to help employers and workers navigate these cliffs, in addition to providing an advocacy platform to reduce the impact of these cliffs on the workforce.

* * *

If there is a silver lining from the dual pandemics of COVID-19 and the devastating impact on the Black and Brown community, it's the spotlight we are now shining on the number of good people in our world who are no longer sitting silently on the sidelines. And I believe there are even more who are willing to step up, stare inequality and injustice in the face, and say, "No more, not on our watch." Together we must pledge to be present, to break down barriers, and to do our part to close gaps. Real change starts in one's own heart. As the gifted young poet Amanda Gorman wrote, "Somehow, we've weathered and witnessed a nation that isn't broken but simply unfinished."[3]

We are a nation whose work is unfinished if we do not live up to our better angels and the ideals of American exceptionalism. I am an example of someone who came from very humble beginnings and through a combination of hard work, perseverance, luck, and the people who opened doors for me and gave me opportunities has been able to change the trajectory of my family's livelihood. But for too many, the American dream is way out of reach, and so the task is to complete that which is unfinished in America.

CHAPTER 7

Meeting the Workforce Challenge

How to Grow the Next Generation
of Healthcare Professionals

A hospital system as large as ours is like managing a city, except we have a singular purpose that requires staying open 365 days a year, 24/7—to be there when people come to us in need of care and in need of healing. In fact, on any given day:

- We will travel to several thousand homes many times, to care for elderly patients with mobility or transportation issues.
- More than 100 babies will take their first breath of life in one of our hospitals.
- Our doctors will perform more than 1,000 surgeries, from appendectomies and hip replacements, lumpectomies and robot-assisted prostatectomies, to heart and liver transplants.
- Thousands will be cared for by our clinicians in one of our outpatient care sites.
- And we will provide up to approximately $5.7 million in free and uncompensated care and other benefits to our communities.

That is just an average day in the life of our healthcare system. We make hundreds of thousands of connections with patients, and in every single one we strive to deliver on our promise of health, hope, and healing.

But if there is something that keeps me up at night, it's thinking about our teammates on the front lines running on that treadmill 24/7, day in and day out, especially during the pandemic. However amazing the groundbreaking technological advances we continue to see, at its core, healthcare is still about real people serving real people. And the stark reality is that there are not enough caregivers nationwide on any particular day to serve the current needs of our communities nationwide. The situation is growing more dire daily, as we face an aging population, which is on pace to double in the next couple of decades.

In 2019, for example, according to an estimate by the Association of American Medical Colleges, the United States had nearly 20,000 fewer doctors than required to meet the country's healthcare needs. At that rate, America is facing a shortage of 124,000 physicians by 2034, including a shortfall of 48,000 primary care doctors.[1] The statistics are equally troubling for medical technologists, pharmacists, respiratory therapists, technicians, assistants, and other healthcare workers—and especially for nurses. The U.S. Bureau of Labor Statistics predicts that each year there will be 195,000 vacancies for registered nurses through 2030.[2]

The nursing problem isn't new. Over the years, nursing shortages have occurred due to economic downturns, increased healthcare demand, and waves of retiring nurses. We're facing the latter scenario once again. In 2020, the median age of RNs was fifty-two, with more than one-fifth planning to retire over the next five years, according to a national survey of the U.S. nursing workforce.[3] And the deficits don't end with RNs. The country is also facing a projected national shortage of more than three million essential health workers,[4] such as certified nursing assistants, patient care assistants, paramedics, security personnel, and environmental services workers.

The burden that the coronavirus pandemic placed on healthcare workers accelerated retirements and career changes among doctors, nurses, technicians, aides, and assistants, which exacerbated the workforce shortages. But stress and overwork were problematic even before COVID-19 hit us.

Gene and Jim Skogsbergh announce the combination of their two organizations, Atrium Health and Advocate Aurora Health, to form one of the largest nonprofit health systems in the country: Advocate Health.

Gene joins as a guest on CBS News' *Face the Nation* with Margaret Brennan to discuss how Atrium Health is deploying resources to tackle the COVID-19 pandemic's disproportionate impact on communities of color.

Gene visits Atrium Health facilities across the Southeast to meet with teammates, helping to boost morale during the COVID-19 pandemic.

Gene and his sister celebrate their First Communion in southern Spain.

Gene's mentor, Tom Robinson, center, was instrumental in his healthcare career.

U.S. Health and Human Services Secretary Alex Azar visits Charlotte, NC, tours Atrium Health's COVID-19 mass testing site at Charlotte Motor Speedway, and meets with Gene and other leaders, including Dr. Jim Hunter, and Dr. David Callaway. U.S. Representative Dan Bishop (R-NC 8th District) was also in attendance.

Dr. David Callaway helped lead Atrium Health's response to the COVID-19 pandemic, embracing the "Fortune Favors the Bold" mantra embroidered on his baseball cap.

Gene and Atrium Health's leadership team break ground on The Pearl Innovation District, which will house the second campus of Wake Forest University School of Medicine. Located in the heart of Charlotte, The Pearl will be a "city within a city" that brings together doctors, scientists, entrepreneurs, academics, and leading life science and medical device companies.

Gene addressing the American Hospital Association in his final meeting as Chair.

In the wake of George Floyd's death, clinicians at Atrium Health join the "White Coats for Black Lives" movement across the country, which aims to dismantle racism in medicine and fight for the health of Black people and other people of color.

Gene and leaders break ground on Atrium Health Union West, a 150,000-square-foot facility with 40 licensed beds and a 24/7 emergency department, to provide better access to top-notch care for rural communities in Union County, North Carolina.

Gene Woods and the Soul Alliance perform at the 2023 Milwaukee Summerfest. The crowd included members of the newly formed Advocate Health executive leadership team and governing board.

Atrium Health partners with Honeywell, Tepper Sports & Entertainment, and Charlotte Motor Speedway to host the largest mass vaccination in the country over a three-day period at Bank of America Stadium, home of the Carolina Panthers and Charlotte Football Club. Over 19,000 first-dose vaccines were administered, serving both drive-through and walk-up traffic.

Dr. Katie Passaretti, enterprise chief epidemiologist at Atrium Health, is pictured receiving her COVID-19 vaccine.

In 2019, the National Academies of Medicine (NAM) reported that burnout had reached "crisis levels, with up to 54 percent of nurses and physicians, and up to 60 percent of medical students and residents, suffering from burnout."[5] The pandemic taxed one group of essential workers particularly hard: respiratory therapists (RTs). A survey of 3,000 RTs at twenty-six U.S. centers in the first three months of 2021 found that 79 percent reported burnout.[6]

In May 2022, Surgeon General Dr. Vivek Murthy issued an advisory, calling attention to the need to address healthcare worker burnout and stressing that it not only harms individual workers but also threatens the entire nation's public health infrastructure. Just as concerning, Dr. Murthy highlighted a national survey conducted in mid-2021 that found eight out of ten healthcare workers experienced at least one type of workplace violence during the pandemic. Another survey showed that two-thirds of healthcare workers have been verbally threatened and one-third of nurses reported an increase in violence, compared to the previous year.

To be sure, healthcare is a high-stakes field that has traditionally attracted those who thrive in high-pressure situations, but the pandemic has turned the heat up to unprecedented levels and affected even the most resilient caregivers. One recent survey of more than 12,000 physicians across a wide range of specialties found that only 49 percent reported being happy, and many were actually clinically depressed.[7]

Although the pandemic had a devastating impact, our teammates persevered through this health crisis with great resolve and dedication to our patients and communities. "Burnout is a very real problem in healthcare," said Scott Rissmiller, MD, our enterprise executive vice president and chief physician executive. "But I will say that our culture was never stronger than it was during those two and a half intense years of the pandemic."

Indeed, our teammates' resilience was remarkable; the way they came together was admirable. But despite their heroics, the pandemic took its toll on them just as it did on health workers in other regions of the country.

"In an ideal world, we would have been able to come out of the pandemic and pause, but we weren't given the opportunity to take that deep breath we all needed because of the reality of the staffing shortages," Dr. Rissmiller said.

A poll commissioned jointly by the Kaiser Family Foundation and the *Washington Post* found that about three in ten healthcare workers considered leaving their profession and about six in ten said they felt their mental health had been compromised by pandemic-related stress.[8] A July 2021 *Nursing Central* survey of thousands of nurses revealed that 91 percent were considering leaving or actively looking to leave the nursing profession.[9]

The Great Resignation

The mass exodus of burned-out workers, driven by the pandemic, has hit healthcare harder than most industries. We were certainly not immune. In 2021, in the Greater Charlotte region alone, we lost 8,842 teammates, many of whom decided to take a break from the workforce, exhausted from the past couple years. That represented approximately 22 percent of our workforce in the region. Fortunately, we were able to weather that challenge and limit further losses due to initiatives started even before the pandemic.

For example, recognizing that one out of five Americans are suffering from mental illness, we have prioritized emotional health support for our teammates, through initiatives such as Help Now, Code Lavender, and our Caregiver Heroes Teammate Emergency Care Fund.

Help Now provides teammates in need of food supplies with a food kit with enough ingredients to feed a family of four for three days. If a teammate needs transportation or child or dependent care in a pinch, we help with that, too. We also provide resources for finding access to lower-cost rental housing and down payment assistance programs, for those wishing to purchase a home. We've created a tool kit of activities and resources for building emotional resilience. Employees can take stress reduction workshops, join a live mindfulness meditation session, and even experience the healing power of music through a free Musicians on Call Music Therapy program.

The Caregiver Heroes Teammate Emergency Care Fund provides teammates with financial assistance, to help when they've suffered hardship caused by catastrophic events beyond their control.

Taking a cue from our hospital emergency system, we've established Code Lavender for any teammate to call when a stressful event occurs.

A team of trained support staff, including members of the chaplaincy department and board-certified holistic nurses, immediately responds with emotional support and other resources. That program to promote teammate resilience has resulted in better teammate satisfaction and retention.

All of these and other actions are part of an overarching initiative called "Best Place to Care." The program began as an effort to foster an organizational culture that empowers physicians to combat work overload, anxiety, depression, and frustration from the amount of paperwork required for every patient.

Best Place to Care isn't just a motivational phrase. It's an intentional movement, with muscle behind it, derived from actively communicating and requesting feedback from our front line. We surveyed doctors, asking, "How are you doing? What can we do better? Where are the friction points that make it more difficult for you to be optimal in your work?"

For example, physicians shared their frustration with the amount of documentation required of them for every patient. It ends up being hours of paperwork, which takes them away from spending more time with patients. We focused on figuring out how to remove unnecessary tasks from the EMR, the electronic medical record, to maximize the clinician's time with the patient. We wanted to become known for empowering physicians to do what they do best for patients in an environment that was focused on also caring for them.

Secondly, we worked to standardize clinical processes, creating evidence-based care pathways that make it easier for doctors to choose the best care options for their patients. We also made a concerted effort toward team-based care, which has been linked to improved patient outcomes and clinician well-being. By coordinating multiple healthcare providers who work collaboratively with patients, we're able to elevate our healthcare professionals to function at the top of their certifications. Too often, we found that our advanced practice providers, like PAs and nurse practitioners, were functioning as glorified scribes rather than true providers of care. And we wanted to empower them to practice at the top of their ability.

The Long and Grinding Road

While we are making strides to address overwork and the burden of mental stress in our teammates, and we are successfully recruiting new staff, the workforce shortages won't go away anytime soon, because it takes years to produce talented healthcare workers. Completing a medical education is a long and grinding road for nurses, therapists, technologists, and especially physicians. Typically, it will take a student entering medical school (after four years as an undergrad) between eight to fifteen years (depending on specialty) to become a practicing physician. Each milestone is fraught with struggle and the possibility of dropping out. And all along that journey, new doctors can rack up big debt. Nearly one in five medical school grads leaves with more than $300,000 in student loan debt, according to the Association of American Medical Colleges.[10]

But it's not just physicians. Behind nearly everything that happens in our hospitals and clinics are unsung heroes called medical laboratory scientists, who perform complex tests on patient samples and report and discuss results with physicians. Today there's a critical shortage of these lab professionals as well, just about one scientist per 1,000 patients, due to retirements and burnout/career changes. And the situation is bound to get worse. A degree takes five years to complete, and the number of lab tech and scientist training programs in the United States has declined nearly 10 percent since 2000.[11]

Aspiring nurses face educational and financial barriers, too. One critical problem contributing to the shortage of nurses is a lack of faculty qualified to teach nursing at the undergraduate level. U.S. nursing schools typically turn away 70,000 to 80,000 qualified applicants yearly from baccalaureate and graduate nursing programs, due to insufficient faculty, classroom space, and budget constraints.

In addition, the average nurse leaves nursing school with upward of $25,000 in student loan debt, which often doesn't include debt acquired in earning an associate or bachelor's degree prior to entering nursing school. While the job is a calling for so many, nurses face long, stressful days filled with emotion and the feeling of being unable to care for yourself after caring for others.

Further, nurses of color can also face unique challenges. I recall hearing from a nurse how often she was mistaken for housekeeping staff.

Another nurse shared the story of a patient who said he refused to be cared for by "a colored person."

Diversity in healthcare leadership and the physician workforce is by no means a new conversation. In 2015, when I chaired the American Hospital Association's committee on Diversity and Health Equity, we launched the #123forEquity pledge campaign, which encouraged health-care organizations to eliminate healthcare disparities and increase diversity in leadership and governance. Leaders of nearly 1,500 of the 5,000 U.S. hospitals signed the pledge.[12] Despite these efforts, hospital leadership and boards remain largely white and male. Minorities represent just 11 percent of executive positions at hospitals, down from 12 percent in 2013. Fewer than 10 percent of hospital CEOs and only 14 percent of board members are minorities, according to the AHA's Institute for Diversity and Health Equity.

The diversity disparity is even more pronounced in the nursing profession. Race and ethnicity statistics indicate that only 9.9 percent of registered nurses are Black or African American, 8.3 percent are Asian, 4.8 percent are Hispanic or Latino, and 0.4 percent are American Indian or Alaskan Native.

The situation is similar among physicians. A recent UCLA study found that the proportion of physicians who are Black in the United States has increased by only four percentage points in 120 years, and the share of doctors who are Black men has not changed since 1940. We find the same conundrum in the fields of physical and occupational therapy and speech pathology and audiology. And enrollment rates for people of color in these programs are far below those of white students. Recently, a version of the Allied Health Workforce Diversity Act (H.R. 3637) was signed into law as part of the year-end 2023 omnibus package. The legislation expands educational opportunities in physical therapy, occupational therapy, respiratory therapy, audiology, and speech-language pathology, including scholarships, stipends, and other activities to boost retention, with a focus on individuals from "disadvantaged backgrounds or individuals who are underrepresented in such professions."

Turning On the Talent Pipeline

Atrium Health has worked hard over the years to buck these trends. Among our 70,000+ teammates, 38 percent are nonwhite and 81 percent are female. We've also leveraged minority- and women-focused programs and strategies to develop and advance emerging leaders. Of promotions to assistant vice president across Atrium Health in recent years, one in two was female and one in five was a person of color. Our teammates engage one another to promote diversity through more than twenty diversity and inclusion councils and system resource groups that include men of color, African American women, teammates interested in faith and spirituality, multicultural physicians, Hispanic/Latino teammates, veterans, and LGBTQ teammates and allies. As a result of these efforts, Atrium Health has been recognized with a number of diversity awards, including *Diversity MBA Magazine*'s "Top Employer" on its list of Best Places to Work for Women and Diverse Managers.

We are proud of these accomplishments, but more needs to be done. We need to expose young people from underrepresented communities to healthcare careers, give them a step stool of experience that leads to jobs, and help them financially and through mentorship to further their education. To that end, Atrium Health has several new and legacy feeder programs like these:

- *Scholarships:* Medical school debt is a barrier to many students from low-income communities, so we committed an initial seeding of $5 million for the Bishop George E. Battle Jr. Scholarship Fund and began a philanthropic campaign dedicated to seeking ongoing support for the scholarship. The money will provide equity in access to those underrepresented students who are pursuing a degree in health sciences at an Atrium Health–affiliated college or university, including Wake Forest University School of Medicine, Carolinas College of Health Sciences, and Cabarrus College of Health Sciences. We expect that scholarship to top $10 million by 2024.
- *Exposure:* Atrium's award-winning PATCH (Propelling Adolescents to Careers in Healthcare) program gives high school

sophomores the opportunity to shadow residents and medical students, to see what healthcare work is really like. PATCH was founded in 2014 by three medical school students who were former teachers in Title One schools. They recognized that low-income students needed role models to spur interest in math and science. The program brings high-achieving high schoolers from local low-income schools to the hospital every Saturday for eight weeks, where medical student leaders give them hands-on clinical training activities, simulation experiences, public health research projects, and one-on-one mentorship. To date, more than 123 PATCH scholars have completed the program, and the overwhelming majority of those surveyed indicated that they plan to attend health professional school and later return to their communities to work.

- *Paid Internships:* Atrium Health participates in MYEP, the Mayor's Youth Employment Program, a paid summer internship for high school juniors that provides training in basic skills in a professional environment and exposure to a possible career pathway.

- *Free Tuition and a Job:* Our Rise to Success initiative is a program that enables high school graduates to earn an associate degree in a healthcare-related field from a local community college while working part-time at our hospital. "We recruit from recent high school grads to come and work for us at Atrium Health, and within a few months they have the skills and competencies to land a healthcare career and an actual job," says Gerard Camacho, Atrium Health's assistant vice president for workforce development. In the program, Atrium Health pays for a participant's tuition and books, in exchange for a commitment to work for us for the duration of their college career and an additional year upon completion of their degree. Atira Chester, a 2020 graduate of Independence High School in Charlotte, says the program gave her the ability to "learn and grow in a field I've always wanted to work, with the bonus of earning money and avoiding student loan debt." Participants are also paired with a career coach who supports their academic and work success and helps them apply to school to earn their bachelor's degree on completion of the program.

These top-level diversity measures trickle down to our healthcare facilities. Studies show that having a hospital workforce that reflects its patients improves measures of health equity and care outcomes. It strengthens doctor-patient trust, makes miscommunication less likely, and promotes greater cultural sensitivity to patient needs, all of which breaks down barriers to healthcare access.

Not long ago, researchers from Penn Medicine in Philadelphia analyzed 117,589 patient surveys (collected following adult outpatient visits across various medical specialties) to explore the relationships between race/ethnicity, gender, and patient experience. Among the questions was one that asked patients the "likelihood of your recommending this care provider to others." The researchers reporting in *JAMA Network Open* found that 87.6 percent of physicians from racially/ethnically concordant patient-physician pairs received the maximum score.

Preference aside, real lives are at stake. A 2021 study published in *JAMA Network Open* assessed mortality rates from 2016 to 2018 and found that the all-cause mortality rate among Black populations was 24 percent higher than among white populations. The report spotlighted the country's pervasive health inequities, with this tragic number: 74,402 more Black people died annually on average than white people during that period. That's more deaths than we'd witness if a 737 jet went down every day for a year—an alarming statistic that should promote outrage. We must get over feeling uncomfortable talking about matters of race.

Getting More Black and Brown People in White Coats

Black or African Americans make up 12.6 percent of people living in the United States but only 5 percent of active U.S. physicians.[13] If, as studies suggest, more Black doctors would improve patient-physician communication and better health outcomes for people of color, then it's obvious that we need more Black doctors.

Why are so few Black students enrolled in medical school? Focus group interviews with African American high school juniors point to these major barriers: financial constraints, lack of knowledge about the medical field, little or no encouragement at home or in school, lack of African American role models in the community and on TV, and racism in medicine.

"I didn't see many Black doctors in my life as a child," says Gary Little, MD, MBA, chief medical officer at Atrium Health. "Knowing that becoming a doctor is achievable as a Black person can be motivating. But if we can't visualize it, if we don't see it, and if there aren't people in your life who can mentor and guide you, then it becomes very difficult to navigate that pathway.

"For me, ignorance was bliss. I guess I benefited from not knowing what I didn't know because I didn't know what I was getting into. Becoming a doctor is just something I thought I could do because I had a propensity for math and science; it came easy to me."

Dr. Little studied premed at Occidental College in Los Angeles, where he said he had a premed advisor who helped him "stay on track" and navigate the process of applying to medical school. Little, who graduated from Harvard Medical School, says an early foundation in math and science and a "drive to study and never be unprepared" are the hallmarks of preparation for success in medical school.

"The numbers of Black males graduating from high school and going to college are very discouraging, and that's the pool you're choosing from to go into medicine, so it's not surprising that there are so few Black men in healthcare," says Dr. Little. "The path really starts even before high school. We've got to prioritize math and science and start students from a very early age."

Mary Nolan Hall, MD, vice chief academic officer, clinical training at Atrium Health, agreed that we are failing to emphasize STEM (science, technology, engineering, and math) skills in elementary school—and not only for African American kids but for everyone. "We're focusing on introducing healthcare careers to high schoolers, which is fine, but the pipeline really begins in third grade; that's where we need to start to build the academic foundation," she says.

It's not that there aren't enough young people with potential but that the educational system isn't designed to nurture it, says Dr. Hall. And clearly the demand for technical talent has never been stronger.

A Comprehensive Academic Enterprise

When Wake Forest Baptist Health combined with Atrium Health in 2022, we embraced the opportunity to create a next-generation academic health system. Our partners in Winston-Salem brought to the table Wake Forest University School of Medicine, with education and research, an MD program, and master's and PhD programs. Atrium Health brought Cabarrus College of Health Sciences, Carolinas College of Health Sciences, plus graduate medical education (GME) programs (residencies and fellowships), and a research component. As I mentioned in the last chapter, together we are building a second campus of the medical school in Charlotte.

Organizing three different degree-granting institutions, two research enterprises, and five sponsoring institutions was a monumental challenge. The task fell to a leadership team led by Julie Ann Freischlag, MD, then chief executive officer of Atrium Health Wake Forest Baptist and chief academic officer of Atrium Health, as well as dean of Wake Forest University School of Medicine, and Terry Hales, executive vice chief academic officer, administration. Their team spent a year designing the health sciences system into an aggregating model that combined clinical, research, and education.

"We cast a vision to position the academic enterprise not as a separate silo but really as the core, the heartbeat of an evolving, academic learning health system," said Hales. "Within that system we have a range of learners, from two-year associate degree nurse's aides and technicians who are a critical part of the hospital workforce, all the way through MDs and PhD research scientists."

(In 2023, Wake Forest University School of Medicine welcomed renowned physician, researcher, and educator Ebony Boulware, MD, as its new dean. Dr. Boulware, who is also chief science officer at Advocate Health, is one of few women medical school deans in the United States. Even though women make up the majority of med students, only 18 percent of deans are women. Only 11 percent of deans are minorities. Fewer still are African American women, like Dr. Boulware.)

We're educating professional healthcare providers along the entire spectrum, 3,200 total learners across more than 100 specialized programs each year. But we have loftier goals than that. As we prepare the future health workforce, we want to be one of the most diverse learner bodies in the country that is representative of the communities we serve and will reduce the shortage of doctors working in inner-city, suburban, and rural areas of the regions we serve. We can't accomplish that goal alone. Because we are a health system deeply entrenched in education, we are at the table, but we need to partner with primary and secondary school educators and local governments, to engineer a series of pipeline programs and relationships that will ensure a more diverse pool of students reaches our doors. Together we can meet the workforce challenges of today and tomorrow, not only in North Carolina but throughout the nation.

CHAPTER 8

The Pearl

Ground Zero for Education, Innovation, and Healing

On historic ground where emancipated slaves settled and built a once prosperous city within a city, a new community is taking shape that will transform the skyline and future of Charlotte forever. Named in honor of the neighborhood's storied Pearl Street Park, Charlotte's first African American park, The Pearl innovation district will be anchored by Wake Forest University School of Medicine, Charlotte's first four-year medical school, and the American headquarters of IRCAD, a global surgical training center specializing in robotics. Interspersed between academic and medical research buildings, and incubator companies on the leading edge of health tech, will be open public spaces, locally owned businesses, a hotel, restaurants, cafés, and entertainment venues. The Pearl is destined to be the crowning jewel of the Queen City.

* * *

The resilience of forests, their remarkable ability to bounce back after being destroyed by wildfire, has always fascinated me. I remember the horrifying wildfires in Yellowstone National Park in 1988 that decimated 793,880 acres, turning that fertile ecosystem into what resembled the aftermath of a nuclear holocaust. Hundreds of bison and elk and other mammals were killed in the fires. Thousands of firefighters, military personnel, and civilians were put in harm's way during what was, at the time, the largest firefighting effort in U.S. history. Yet despite the carnage, something good eventually came out of those devastating fires. When the snows finally cooled the scorched earth, sunlight, which hadn't been able to reach the forest floor for decades, due to tree cover, coaxed seeds in the soil to germinate. The ash left by the inferno enriched the soil with minerals to fertilize their growth. Basal buds sprouted from the trunks of dead trees. And in the spring of 1989, less than a year after the last embers were extinguished, the nation witnessed the rebirth of the forest in the incredible display of wildflowers that graced Yellowstone. Ultimately, Yellowstone's forest environment became healthier, thanks to the devastation that once razed it.

In many ways, I see an analogous transformation occurring in Charlotte's Second Ward, which encompasses the neighborhood formerly known as Brooklyn. We plan to transform the area into a booming hub for health sciences education and cutting-edge medical research within a dynamic, livable neighborhood. The Pearl innovation district, on thirty acres near downtown Charlotte, is a project meant to rejuvenate a historic neighborhood with a medical school and other educational opportunities, world-class life sciences companies, and high-tech startups interspersed with locally owned businesses, cafés, restaurants, shops, open community spaces, and affordable housing. In the coming years, it will create more than 10,000 new jobs, many of which will not require a bachelor's degree.

Brooklyn was once a prosperous African American community, a bustling city within a city, with thriving Black-owned businesses, places of worship, and Charlotte's first high school to open to Black students. But in the 1960s, Brooklyn was ravaged, not by a forest fire, but by something equally devastating to its residents: urban renewal, the government's deeply flawed program to revitalize blighted areas in cities across the United States.

In an interview following his historic 1963 meeting with Attorney General Robert Kennedy, the novelist James Baldwin described this misguided inner-city face-lifting in the simplest of terms: "Urban renewal is Negro removal.["1] And that's how many residents from Brooklyn felt. What was intended to eliminate slum housing, reduce segregation, and recharge the local economy resulted in the displacement of more than 1,000 low- and moderate-income families, the destruction of historic structures, and the closing of twelve churches and 200 small businesses. The wounds were deep.

The Rev. Janet Garner-Mullins remembers growing up in historic Brooklyn during the Jim Crow era and recalls the devastating impact of displacement, which still stings for many in the city today. "The entire community was torn down, bulldozed for what was called urban renewal, which uprooted the lives of Black people, Black businesses, and Black churches," she told WCCB-TV in Charlotte.[2] Many, many Charlotteans share her memories and continue to deal with the emotional consequences of displacement. A former Brooklyn resident we spoke with told the story of standing on the sidewalk and watching the house she grew up in being razed. She told us that the scene of the crane with a wrecking ball pounding the brick into a cloud of dust has remained with her and is as fresh as the day it happened some sixty years ago.

These are the kinds of scars that don't fade. And the trauma folks experienced in Brooklyn wasn't confined to Charlotte. It was endemic in cities throughout the country.

The displacement of low-income households is a story that has been repeated time and time again throughout this nation. And it continues today, only now it's called gentrification. A study by the National Community Reinvestment Coalition looked at more than 1,000 neighborhoods in 935 cities and towns where gentrification had occurred between 2000 and 2013 and found that rapidly rising rents, property values, and taxes forced 135,000 residents to move away.[3] Gentrification often also leads to cultural displacement, because the longtime residents who are dispersed are typically people of color. And those communities that are lost are rarely reunited.

More than three decades before urban renewal, a different type of government program discriminated against our Black and Brown communities through a practice called "redlining." Real estate agents and banks, working for the newly created Federal Housing Administration, began rating neighborhoods according to the risks they posed to lenders.

They created color-coded maps, outlining minority neighborhoods in red, meaning "hazardous to lenders," which made it impossible for people living there to get mortgages to buy homes or loans to improve properties. The practice ultimately led to the decay of once-thriving communities.

"Redlining created the crisis that urban renewal was created to solve," says Brent Cebul, PhD, an urban historian at the University of Pennsylvania and lead investigator for *Renewing Inequality: Family Displacements through Urban Renewal, 1950–1966,* part of the American Panorama digital historical atlas.[4]

The Fair Housing Act of 1968 made it unlawful for lenders to "discriminate against any person because of race, color, sex, handicap or religion," but redlining has left a legacy of inequity in economic mobility and opportunity. Without a doubt, it has contributed to the vast gulf in wealth between people of color and whites today, because homeownership is such a powerful driver of wealth creation. And we are still living with the visible vestiges of redlining. The neighborhoods where African Americans were allowed to live are food deserts, they lack good schools, they are missing other infrastructure components of economic mobility, and they keep residents in poverty for generations. The negative impact doesn't end with economics. Research has linked historic redlining with a host of health risks for Black and Hispanic residents, including higher levels of premature death, overall mortality, infant mortality, and chronic diseases like cancer, asthma, heart disease, mental health disorders, and type 2 diabetes.[5] In fact, the legacy of previously redlined communities is that often there can be a fifteen- to thirty-year life expectancy gap between these communities and the more affluent communities sometimes only a few minutes' drive away.

A Tale of Two Cities

The damaging past practices of redlining and displacement begged those of us planning The Pearl to ask hard questions today: How do we avoid repeating the mistakes of the past? So many people in Charlotte either lived in Brooklyn or had a historical connection to that community through family, businesses, or place of worship. How do we help them heal? How do we deliver to descendants the economic opportunities that their grandparents were denied? How do we create "inclusive renewal," through innovation and growth, to ensure that all take part in and thrive as a result of The Pearl's success?

As we wrestled with those important questions, I was reminded of a keynote address that former Bank of America CEO and Chairman Hugh McColl gave to the Echo Foundation in 2019. Hugh was the first to create a national, coast-to-coast bank. He acquired seventy-five banks in Florida to merge into his North Carolina National Bank (NCNB) in 1992, when cross-state banking was not allowed. Through McColl's dogged lobbying of members of Congress, Congress in 1994 finally allowed banks to own other banks across state lines. Four years later, McColl pulled off an unprecedented $66.6 million merger of NCNB with BankAmerica to create Charlotte-based Bank of America, now the second-largest financial institution in the world. Of note, Ed Brown, who would later become the Atrium Health board chair, was one of his key lieutenants during that time.

While McColl was building a bank, he was also instrumental in building a city—Charlotte.

"It used to be that you could fire a shotgun down the street at five in the afternoon and not hit anybody; that's how boring this town was," McColl told *Our State* magazine in 2017. "You need the arts, you need pro sports, you need the whole nine yards." [6]

And McColl proceeded to get those first downs, driving growth in the form of schools, museums, a thriving arts and entertainment community, with theaters and performance halls that include his beloved Charlotte Ballet, exciting sports facilities, and the businesses, restaurants, and hotels that support it all. McColl and his contemporaries in Charlotte leadership built an envied model of the New South.

But in his speech that night, McColl told the tale of *two* cities, "the city we built and the city we didn't build."

"What we have not yet built," he declared, "is a city that shares opportunity equally for all its people . . . a city of racial progress and reconciliation. That's the work that is yet to be done."

In typical McColl fashion, Hugh did not end his address without suggesting a prescription for how to build that new city within a city. "It is well past time for a new humility," he told the crowd at the Echo Foundation, "for deep listening, for sustained and intentional actions that will spread opportunity throughout the city to all our neighbors. When we fail to bring opportunity to all our citizens, our entire city suffers. When we fail to develop the talents, skills, and leadership potential of all our citizens, we neglect our most vital resource as a community . . . our people."

Our people. That's the resource that will be most critical to the success of The Pearl innovation district, the foundation for our grand plans. It became clear to us that to compete on the national stage and drive innovation in clinical and research excellence, we must be forward-looking and bold about our workforce and talent pipeline. There's no doubt that The Pearl innovation district is the right idea at the right time for new beginnings for this community. When complete, The Pearl, which is being built by Atrium Health, in partnership with developer Wexford Science & Technology, will be a place where Charlotte's historic vitality meets its innovative future. But to achieve that end and avoid the mistakes of the past, we realized we needed to keep the community at the heart of the project. We had to become a national model for inclusive growth. So, we embarked on a number of approaches to do that. For one, we established a community advisory board made up of people who live in the communities around this district that helped cocreate the design of The Pearl. We engaged another group of citizens to develop the Brooklyn Purposeful Walk, a marked trail where visitors can explore the history of old Brooklyn, so we don't forget what was once there. It's a touchstone to remind us that The Pearl must represent inclusive growth. Its goal must be to elevate the community through job creation and innovation, as we forge a path to revolutionizing healthcare.

Creation of a Pearl

What's so appealing about Brooklyn, in what is now known as Charlotte's Second Ward, is its authenticity, its heritage, and, particularly, its significance to the history of healthcare in the United States. Just blocks from the area of Brooklyn, near what's now Bank of America Stadium in the Third Ward, stood Good Samaritan Hospital, the first privately funded, independent hospital built exclusively for the treatment of Blacks in North Carolina.[7] And at the time it was the only hospital allowing Black physicians and nurses to practice. The building, constructed with funds raised through St. Peter's Episcopal Church and by private donors, was dedicated on September 23, 1891. The following morning's newspaper, the *Charlotte Evening Chronicle*, described it as "one of the most conveniently arranged buildings that could be built for [the exclusive use of colored people], and every room is well ventilated. On the upper and lower floors are hot and cold baths, and the rooms are provided with iron cots with springs."[8] In 1903, the hospital established a nursing school, to give local women further career opportunities. According to a 1929 survey by the American Medical Association, Good Sam, as it was affectionately known, was one of the oldest Black hospitals in operation in the entire United States at the time. Only the Georgia Infirmary in Savannah (1832), Freeman's Hospital in Washington, D.C. (1865), Prince George's House of Reformation in Cheltenham, Maryland (1872), and Central Hospital in Petersburg, Virginia (1870) predated Good Samaritan. Interestingly, Central Hospital was a predecessor of the hospital where I held my first vice president role in Petersburg.[9]

Good Sam hospital fell into disrepair and was sold to the city and reopened as Charlotte Community Hospital in 1961. The building was demolished in 1996, but the hospital chapel was saved to ensure we never forget this history. Fortuitously we were able to procure that chapel, which will be preserved at The Pearl—as a homage to the past.

The neighborhoods that Good Sam hospital once served will be home to a second campus of Wake Forest University School of Medicine. Built on a twenty-acre site at McDowell and Baxter streets and adjacent to US-277, the School of Medicine is very near Atrium Health Carolinas Medical Center and within eyesight of Charlotte's uptown area. It'll be a place filled with all sorts of experiential learning spaces and opportunities for a diverse population of students to interact. The medical school's Howard R. Levine Center for Education campus will also house Wake Forest University School of Professional Studies, Carolinas College of Health Sciences, and other educational opportunities in The Pearl. Nearby Johnson C. Smith University, a historically Black college, will serve as one of many feeder universities for certified nurse's aides, medical students, technicians, and business students who will find educational and job possibilities right in their own backyards.

"Charlotte's campus provides students with some of the finest minds in academia," says Dr. Julie Freischlag chief academic officer for Advocate Health, CEO of Atrium Health Wake Forest Baptist, and executive vice president for health affairs, Wake Forest University. "School of Medicine students and residents both have easy access to the renowned experts practicing at our combined world-class service lines across multiple specialties."

A Connected Corridor of Innovation

Dr. Freischlag is referring to the geographic link that will be created between the two medical school campuses, one in Winston-Salem's renowned Innovation Quarter and the other in Charlotte's The Pearl innovation district, a corridor that will become a magnet for best-in-class healthcare businesses, research and development facilities, and health tech startups. I envision it becoming the Silicon Valley for cutting-edge health science in the nation, which will drive our capability to improve community health, wellness, and prevention. The corridor also will provide advanced learning and spur economic growth and opportunity for the entire state and region.

The connection between Winston-Salem and Charlotte will be seamless, through Atrium Health's alliance with Wexford Science & Technology. Wexford, in partnership with Wake Forest Baptist Health, government, local businesses, and community members, planned and developed Winston-Salem's Innovation Quarter, a 2.1-million-square-foot mixed-use community and home to Wake Forest University School of Medicine, built on the former site of the R. J. Reynolds Tobacco Co.

It's a remarkable story of transformation. Before its inception, Winston-Salem was losing jobs. Banks and businesses were fleeing. Yet here, built on the literal stone foundations of an industry linked to lung cancer, emerged a new industry dedicated to fighting cancer and other diseases, such as Alzheimer's disease, cardiovascular disease, and more, while promoting health, healing, and education.

In 2020, the Innovation Quarter gained the distinction of "Best Practice for Creating Integrated Places" by the Global Institute on Innovation Districts. It's a vibrant 330-acre community in thriving downtown Winston-Salem, where thousands of workers and students enjoy urban green spaces, restaurants, coffee shops, food trucks, lunchtime concerts in the park—and affordable housing. The Innovation Quarter has been a boon to the city, attracting dozens of new tech and health sciences businesses and high-level talent. The Quarter and the entire city gained even more workers during the pandemic, as people left the big cities in search of a better quality of life.

Not far from Atrium Health Wake Forest Baptist Medical Center, the Innovation Quarter is anchored by Wake Forest University School of Medicine's Bowman Gray Center for Medical Education, housed in the former Reynolds Tobacco manufacturing plant. It's a place that is transforming medical education, with clinical simulation labs and collaborative learning spaces, where students advance their biomedical knowledge, gain technical investigative skills, and develop the essential humanistic elements of medicine. In other words, said Dr. Freischlag, "The ways we communicate compassion and caring for patients because patient and family-centered care is a driving force of our learning philosophy."

The Innovation Quarter is also home to Wake Forest Institute of Regenerative Medicine (WFIRM). The U.S. Department of Health and Human Services calls regenerative medicine "the next evolution of medical treatments." (I like to think of it as the next evolution of cures.) RM is the science of growing new human cells, tissues, and organs in a laboratory for repair or transplantation, bringing new hope to the more than 100,000 in the United States who are currently waiting for a lifesaving organ transplant. WFIRM is led by the brilliant scientist Dr. Anthony Atala, who was named by *Scientific American* as one of the most influential people in biotechnology. And that's just one of dozens of accolades Atala and WFIRM researchers have garnered. His team of physicians and scientists were the first in the world to engineer lab-grown tissues and organs, such as skin, cartilage, bladders, muscle, and even solid organs like kidneys that have been successfully used in human patients. WFIRM even uses 3D printing techniques to fabricate complex scaffolds, by stacking printed materials layer by layer. It's on these bioprinted structures that scientists grow cartilage, heart valves, liver tissue, and skin that will be used to replace diseased and injured organs. It's a process of transformation that is redefining how we heal the human body, and the institute's influence is far-reaching. It collaborates with academic and medical industry entities worldwide, on breakthrough research in diagnostics, drug discovery, biomanufacturing, nanotechnology, and gene editing.

Roughly eighty miles south of the Innovation Quarter, The Pearl innovation district will be home to its own transformative research institute, the U.S. headquarters of IRCAD. That stands for, in French, "Institut de Recherche contre les Cancers de l'Appareil Digestif," the Institute for Research into Cancer of the Digestive System. With world headquarters in Strasbourg, France, IRCAD specializes in educating physicians from around the world in minimally invasive surgery techniques. A big part of its business is research and development in computer science and surgical robotics, as well as other tools for diagnosis, and surgical planning, simulation, and training, all aimed at making surgical procedures more precise and safer. IRCAD has now expanded to six training centers in five countries. The Charlotte site will be IRCAD's North American headquarters, a premier site to train surgeons in one of eighteen specialties in laparoscopic, flexible, and robotic surgery.

I traveled to Strasbourg to see IRCAD's operation firsthand and met with its founder, the famed French surgeon Jacques Marescaux. A soft-spoken, yet charismatic visionary, Marescaux met me with a smile, wearing his trademark hospital scrubs, to take me through glass-enclosed surgical bays, where doctors from around the world were learning the latest robotic surgery techniques. Marescaux, a brilliant scientist, is also a Renaissance man from the French countryside who loves art and music and can connect equally with paupers and kings. When we shook hands, I noticed his hands—rougher than I expected a surgeon's to be, but clearly skilled. Marescaux and his team successfully performed the first ever no-scar surgery, an incisionless operation using an endoscope. He was instrumental in orchestrating the world's first trans-Atlantic surgery (surgeons in New York, patient in France), performed via fiber optics that were linked to a robot. As we watched surgeons from Uganda to Ukraine practicing together with IRCAD's high-tech tools in Strasbourg, it felt like he was orchestrating a world community, to help teach and heal people from around the globe. And Dr. Marescaux's greatest legacy may be bridging the chasms created by war and conflict by exporting advanced medical techniques throughout the world.

"Together we can create the future of medicine right here, right now," he told me before I left Strasbourg, and I knew that what we were embarking on with IRCAD in Charlotte would be among the most transformative initiatives that I would be part of in my entire career.

IRCAD's presence has become a supermagnet for luring a portfolio of life sciences and health science companies to The Pearl. Leading global medical technology manufacturers like Siemens Healthineers have become strategic partners with IRCAD in the innovation district, further elevating The Pearl's profile and catapulting North Carolina even higher among states with top-tier capabilities for clinical research and innovation.

Bringing IRCAD to Charlotte is another shining example of what's needed to truly transform healthcare in the United States—a partnership that involves not-for-profit health systems, private industry, and elected government officials working in lockstep toward a common goal. The Pearl and its flagships, IRCAD and Wake Forest University School of Medicine, are products of a strong partnership with the City of Charlotte, Mecklenburg County, and the state of North Carolina, thanks to leaders who recognized the inclusive economic growth that will come from advancing health science education, fostering research and development, and incubating new businesses. The city and county have committed $75 million in tax increment grants and capital improvement bonds, which will pay for infrastructure improvements to the site, including walking and biking paths. In return for the city and county's investment, we contributed to the city fourteen acres of prime real estate, to use for affordable housing—something that had never been done in the history of Charlotte. This was an example of trying to heal the wounds of the past, specifically the displacement of Black families in the adjacent Brooklyn community. Our intention is for our significant investments in The Pearl to not displace families but instead allow them live, work, and play near The Pearl so that they can participate in the economic mobility it will bring.

The civic investment was contingent upon Atrium Health and Wexford securing private investment that would start generating tax revenue. Ultimately, the project will net Mecklenburg County $43.6 million in tax revenue over a twenty-year span, all from a parcel of land that previously generated no tax dollars. Ninety percent of that new revenue is expected to pay for other critical public needs.

One project I'm particularly excited about, funded by local government investment, is an open-air, stepped plaza that takes its design inspiration from an iconic structure in old Brooklyn called Jacob's Ladder. Biblically named, Jacob's Ladder was a series of tenement fire escapes on which young people would gather to sing hymns and gospel songs, back in the day. One observer noted, "The children would line up along the stairs and sing hymns; to the community this was representative of angels ascending to heaven, and a symbol for the neighborhood of the betterment of the community through education, uplifting each other out of poverty, and congregating to support one another." That is the perfect description of what we were striving to do not just at The Pearl but throughout our health system. Similarly, the plaza will become a place where people gather to engage and, yes, maybe strum a guitar and belt out a tune, just as in Brooklyn's heyday.

This innovation corridor is a model for growth that promises to lift all ships and help provide health, healing, and hope for everyone in the region. In just the few months following the announcement of our plans for The Pearl, we heard from more than 100 companies that were interested in planting their flag in Charlotte's soil and becoming a part of this vibrant ecosystem of health.

Thomas Osha, executive vice president for Wexford Science & Technology, called The Pearl "an innovation ecosystem that is grounded in research and academics [that] will include corporate innovators, incubate new ideas and businesses, attract venture funding, and scale growth businesses, particularly minority-owned ventures, into a geography where these assets and attributes are amplified for innovation, community, and economic impact."

And within the next fifteen years, we anticipate The Pearl and its tenants will create more than 5,500 on-site jobs, 40 percent of which are not expected to require a college degree, and more than 11,500 jobs in the Charlotte region. Many of those jobs will be a direct result of the healthcare sector talent pipeline that we're priming, including through the Bishop Battle scholarship and other programs targeting underrepresented communities.

What The Pearl Will Do for Our Sabrinas

The Pearl innovation district sets in motion our ability to grow and evolve healthcare over the next 100 years. From it will emerge lifesaving medical technologies that we can only dream about today, which will impact all of humanity in the decades to come.

That said, what I am most excited about is what The Pearl will mean for a young girl—let's call her Sabrina—living in the neighborhood of McCrorey Heights and the thousands of children like her who deserve a more secure future.

I introduced "Sabrina" to the Atrium Health board of directors during a meeting to update them on progress at The Pearl, as a way to illuminate the difference we will make in people's lives. Ten-year-old Sabrina was not there physically because she's a composite, a representation of the bright, smiling, eager youth of a Charlotte-Mecklenburg public school called Bruns Avenue Elementary in McCrorey Heights.

Sabrina's story is fiction, but her situation isn't. Bruns Elementary is a Title One school, where most students qualify for free or reduced lunch.

This is how we envision helping the Sabrinas in the community: Sabrina is mentored and nurtured by teachers working hard to give their students a bright future. She loves school and does well in her classes. Sabrina's mom, Jasmine, is a single parent, who works hard at two jobs and cares for Sabrina and her younger brother, Robert. Jasmine appreciates the fact that she doesn't have to miss work to take her daughter to a doctor's appointment for an ear infection, because Atrium Health doctors provide virtual primary care to all the students at Sabrina's school.

Jasmine learns more about Atrium Health, while chaperoning her daughter's class on a field trip to The Pearl innovation district, where they see cutting-edge robotics and surgical technology. She picks up a flyer announcing free STEM classes for nine- and ten-year-olds and shows it to Sabrina, who has always talked about becoming a doctor. She's good at math and loves her science class, Jasmine thinks, but she really needs more, and this STEM class offers hands-on labs.

Sabrina's ear-to-ear smile cements the deal. Jasmine signs her daughter up.

A few weeks in, Jasmine drops Sabrina off at class. While passing the time, walking through The Pearl with her son Robert, she spots a job posting on her phone. It's at one of the medical research buildings just around the corner.

She walks in and applies. Two interviews later, she lands the job. It comes with a significantly higher paycheck (with benefits) that allows her to drop her second job.

Fast-forward five years: Sabrina is now in high school, a solid A-B student. Her AP biology teacher tells her class about a local opportunity to explore healthcare careers. It's called Atrium Health's PATCH, for Propelling Adolescents to Careers in Healthcare. Founded by three medical students, the program is designed to expose underrepresented minority high schoolers to healthcare careers. Students visit hospitals and shadow medical students and doctors on nine consecutive Saturdays. What's more, the residents really get to know the kids and become mentors, encouraging these talented young people to pursue their dreams. Sabrina stays after school to ask her teacher for an application.

Jump to high school graduation: Sabrina's time in the PATCH program has confirmed her childhood dream of becoming a doctor. She wants to be a pediatrician. She'd love to help the kids in her old elementary school one day. So, she applies and is accepted to Johnson C. Smith University, right in town. Earning the Bishop George E. Battle Scholarship at JSCU to help fund her education plays a chief role in her college choice, and besides, she's eager to remain close to home and to her mom and brother.

Sabrina enters a premed program. By the beginning of her junior year, she's offered a paid internship at Atrium Health Carolinas Medical Center, recording patient histories as a nurse's helper. It doesn't take long for the friendly teen to negotiate regular visits to nearby Levine Children's Hospital, where she shadows doctors in the pediatric emergency department.

The next chapter: Sabrina is accepted at three medical schools. More decisions to make. But you can bet she'll make the right one, again by staying in Charlotte and at Atrium Health, to pay it forward to the next generation of Sabrinas and to be an example of what is possible.

This is part of our solution to the problem of there being too few doctors and nurses, lab technicians, pharmacists, and therapists—including from underrepresented groups. We are focused on helping the many

Sabrinas, Lucias, Dions, Roberts, and Santiagos who choose careers in healthcare to have opportunities with us and serve the communities where they grew up. And we will ensure that they have the necessary tools and training to be successful. They'll benefit from the effective partnerships we have built between private enterprise, local government, and community organizations that are committed to building the city that Hugh McColl said we forgot to build. Ours is a tide that lifts all boats.

As I was writing this book, I met up with Hugh McColl at a function in town. He pulled me aside and said, "Gene, I believe The Pearl will be the most important thing that ever happened to the Charlotte region, and it will transform healthcare nationally. It will help bring the tale of two cities into one that lifted up everyone."

This from a visionary leader who created the first national bank headquarters in Charlotte, which put the city on the map. It was extraordinarily humbling to hear that from the man who built Bank of America. I pictured a natural pearl formed by the methodical layering of nacre over time. And I smiled, thinking of Sabrina, and feeling confident that a new city within a city is rising again.

CHAPTER 9

How Healthcare Works in America

Recently, a doctor friend of mine explained why he doesn't enjoy flying so much:

"When my seatmates find out I'm a physician, they invariably pump me for doctorly advice," he said. "Once on a flight to LA, a guy asked me to diagnose the mole on his hand."

That's an occupational hazard of being a physician.

I'm asked a different type of question on flights and at parties when people learn my line of work. (By the way, I get these from friends and family, too, especially my sons!)

Why are hospital stays so expensive?

How can an aspirin cost thirty dollars?

I had an operation and couldn't make heads or tails of my hospital statement. Why can't it be more like an auto repair bill?

Why won't my insurance pay for this?

My typical response usually gets a chuckle: "Hmm, got a few hours?"

But seriously, it would take *more* than a few hours to do justice to those queries and to even begin to part the clouds of opacity on healthcare costs. The healthcare industry is a very complex operation, one that we would frankly never design this way, if we were to start over with a blank sheet. It's a system with so many undulating tentacles, it's no wonder consumers scratch their heads and throw up their hands in frustration.

I get it. When my father was diagnosed with multiple myeloma, I spent many hours helping him sort out the many hospital bills and insurance company EOBs (explanations of benefits). But it is important to unpack this, because it affects us individually and collectively. The United States spends more than $4 trillion of our gross domestic product on healthcare, almost $13,000 per person annually.[1]

To extend the Q&A analogy, how do I explain something so complex as hospital finance to someone who doesn't have my thirty years of hospital and healthcare experience? How do I keep their eyes from glazing over before the plane lands?

The simple answer doesn't exist in the age of the internet news feed. You can't tell the story in one sentence, but that's often all we have to work with.

Blame it all on the first nationally televised presidential debate in 1960—John Fitzgerald Kennedy versus Richard Milhous Nixon. That debate forever transformed the thirteen-inch newspaper column into a sound bite. At the time of Nixon's successful bid for the White House in '68, the length of a sound bite from a presidential candidate averaged 42.3 seconds. Today, thanks to digital and social media, it has shrunk to around seven seconds.[2] Or a 280-character tweet.

Tweets and sound bites rarely lead to better understanding. One survey, for example, found that 35 percent of people are not aware that Obamacare and the Affordable Care Act are the same thing. And nearly one-third believe Obamacare had been repealed![3]

Here's another example, from a Kaiser Family Foundation (KFF) poll released in the spring of 2022: among Americans with private health insurance, the survey found that 56 percent said they had never heard of the No Surprises Act, a law that protects people with private health insurance from getting large medical bills when they accidentally receive out-of-network healthcare.[4]

Clearly there is a fundamental gap in communication and understanding. And it's simply impossible to explain the challenges of affordability and the complexity of healthcare finance in a seven-second-long media sound bite.

And yet it is absolutely essential that people understand, at a minimum, Healthcare Financing 101, since affordability is clearly top of mind for most Americans. That same KFF survey found that Americans' biggest healthcare concern continues to be affordability. The poll also revealed that 61 percent of the population believe that Congress should prioritize limiting how much drug companies can raise prices for prescription medications each year to no more than the rate of inflation. And 42 percent of those surveyed said Medicaid access should be expanded.

People want solutions. They have valid questions. And their misconceptions about the healthcare cost structure are often formed by social media posts, biased blogs, and quick sound bites that lack context. Is it any surprise, then, that we hear comments like:

> We need cost transparency.
> Can't we make healthcare more affordable?
> It must be nice to be able to set prices to meet your budget.

While hospital systems like ours do our best to provide the tools to help folks know the cost of their care, it's obviously a challenge. Most American families have seen medical care prices and insurance premiums grow faster than their wages. To begin to fathom why, and to recognize the challenge that the healthcare industry faces, it may help to understand how hospitals are reimbursed for care, and how nonprofit health systems spend their resources.

In this book, fortunately, I have the luxury of offering a much longer sound bite than most.

We're Price Takers . . .

First, let's clear up the misunderstanding that nonprofit hospitals set prices to our liking. It just doesn't happen that way. We're essentially price takers, not price setters. The market, influenced by rising drug prices and insurance rates (and inflation), determines what each patient is charged. We must accept the prevailing prices in the marketplace; how we do our daily work has little effect on how many dollars you pay out of pocket.

It's critical to understand that many hospital systems like ours have no control over the prices that account for more than 60 percent of our revenue. They're set in concrete. In our case, most of that reimbursement comes from the federal government, the Centers for Medicare and

Medicaid Services (CMS), which sets our prices. An additional 10 percent of that is provided to those who are uninsured and can't afford to pay. To provide a snapshot, in 2022, we provided:

- Over $437 million in care to more than 100,000 low-income, uninsured patients who never received a bill for the care they received.
- Automatic discounts to more than 160,000 uninsured patients, totaling $150 million.
- More than $11 million in discounts through our Hardship Settlement Program.

That leaves about 30 percent of our revenue from insurance companies, where the annual increases we receive do not cover the significant inflation we have experienced. Our costs have increased by more than 15 percent, due to pandemic-fueled inflation, worker shortages, supply chain disruptions, and rising drug expenses. To add a finer point, those labor costs used to be approximately 55 percent of total revenues; today they're approaching 70 percent. Because of these pressures, in 2022, half of the nation's hospitals were operating in the red.

That math demonstrates how the current scenario is not sustainable. Total hospital Medicare margins have dropped precipitously since 2010 and will likely continue to do so. Nationally, combined Medicare and Medicaid reimbursements fell $100 billion short of the actual costs of care in 2020, up from $75.8 billion in 2019. Because CMS payments are fixed, hospitals are unable to absorb the inflationary forces affecting them. So, the notion in some media reports that nonprofit hospital systems profit from Medicare due to their tax-exempt status is false. Atrium Health alone, for example, lost $1.1 billion in 2021 by serving Medicare patients. And, generally speaking, Medicaid reimbursement rates are significantly lower than those of Medicare by two-thirds. As the largest safety net provider of Medicaid in the state of North Carolina, for example, and among the top twenty nationally, this has a disproportionate impact on our organization.

As health systems struggle with these challenges, health insurance and pharmaceutical companies are thriving. The seven largest insurers posted record profits, totaling roughly $23 billion in the third quarter of 2022, at a time when health systems experienced the worst financials in a decade.

Code Red

In addition to these financial challenges, we also devote millions and millions of dollars in resources and staff, to comply with the onerous regulatory burden that has been created by the government and insurance companies, so that we may be reimbursed for the lifesaving care we provide. These reimbursement protocols are based on disease and medical procedure codes called the ICD-10, or International Classification of Diseases 10th Revision code, and the HCPCS, or Healthcare Common Procedure Coding System codes, respectively. Here's an example: a type 2 diabetes diagnosis is coded as ICD-10 E11, and a glucose tolerance test is code HCPCS101200. I'm sure you'd agree that's a mouthful.

So, when billing for services, we have to decide which is the right billing code from among 69,000 of these ICD-10 inpatient codes, clumped into 750 Diagnosis-Related Groups, or DRGs, plus 16,400 outpatient HCPCS codes, grouped into 740 ambulatory payment classifications, or APCs. As I said, if we were building this system from scratch, we certainly wouldn't do it this way! This administrative burden falls many times on clinicians whose time would be better spent attending to patients than on the incredibly complex paperwork required to match obscure codes to a particular diagnosis. And, as you might imagine, it's an alphabet soup of documentation mistakes waiting to happen. If a doctor in a hectic emergency room doesn't also include all the correct written information, Medicare may deny payment for care that was already provided to that patient.

In addition to the complexity of dealing with Medicare/Medicaid, private insurance billing can be just as cumbersome. It's also not uncommon for a hospital system to engage with hundreds of commercial insurance plans, each with a unique benefit design and payment model.

Perhaps more frustrating is what is called "prior authorization," the need to get approval from the patient's insurance company before medical care can be provided. The American Medical Association did a survey in 2021 and found that one out of three physicians said that delays in getting approval caused patients significant harm and even death.[5] Clearly the paperwork required to care for our patients has completely gotten out of hand, and it adds significantly to the cost burden.

This is a window into how healthcare works in America. Suffice it to say, again, that if we were to design the healthcare system from scratch today, it would never look like this.

That said, healthcare systems want and must certainly be part of the solution and continue to drive down costs. For example, we have been able to save hundreds of millions in overhead due to the efficiencies we have achieved, but it is important to understand the systemic challenges that can't be boiled down to a tweet. And, time and time again, I have seen communities spiral downward when their local hospital closes because of these challenges, especially in rural communities. In fact, according to the America Hospital Association, between 2010 and 2021, 136 rural hospitals shut their doors. Another 600 hospitals are on the verge of doing the same. In communities where a hospital has closed, residents must now sometimes drive for hours to get lifesaving care. That in and of itself is the compelling reason for why we must change the system. It is ailing and in need of serious intervention.

Walking the Talk

Atrium Health is one of the top safety-net providers in the country, and we've recently combined with another top healthcare system, Advocate Aurora Health. Collectively, we deliver nearly $5 billion in community benefits.

But what exactly does "community benefit" mean? Besides uncompensated Medicare and Medicaid care, bad debt costs from patients who do not pay for services, and financial assistance to uninsured patients, we contribute tens of millions of dollars to community-building activities, medical education and research, and cash and in-kind donations to local nonprofits and charities. A terrific illustration of community benefit is what we're doing in Charlotte's oldest surviving Black neighborhood, Biddleville, home of the city's historically Black college, Johnson C. Smith University. Atrium Health's Biddle Point Family Practice is a vibrant city clinic, receiving more than 22,500 visits annually and serving a neighborhood that faces such common urban health and social problems as homelessness, violence, AIDS, teenage pregnancy, and food insecurity. Forty-eight percent of Biddle Point's patients are either uninsured or on Medicaid.

Established in 1996, the Biddle Point facility grew out of a partnership between the Department of Family Medicine at Carolinas Medical Center and community leaders, with the goal of bringing quality healthcare to Biddleville's underserved population. Today, it's a national model for community-based healthcare, with programs customized to the neighborhood's needs. There's a full-time social worker and pregnancy case manager, a full pharmacy with lower-priced prescriptions and education programs, specialty HIV treatment and programming, a pediatric dental clinic, screening for social determinants of health, and a Reach Out and Read program that creates reading and other language-rich activities for young children to foster healthy brain development and help families build meaningful bonds. Biddle Point Clinic also features one of Atrium Health's two mobile food pharmacies, which travel to neighborhoods identified as food deserts that lack access to fresh, nutritious, affordable food. This is a critical step toward addressing the social determinants of health, because we know that access to nutritious food improves a person's overall health and ability to thrive in school or in the workplace.

Another initiative unique to the Atrium Health Biddle Point practice is an Urban Track Family Medicine Residency Program, for medical students who aspire to work in urban settings helping an underserved, financially insecure population. Residencies like this are desperately needed, to train medical students to fill workforce shortages in community-oriented primary care, disease prevention, and geriatrics in urban areas like Biddleville. They result in more physicians who are driven and dedicated to these growing needs and are often staffed by physicians who grew up in those same neighborhoods.

The Eye of the Storm

As we lick our wounds from the COVID-19 battle, we can't pine for the pre-pandemic days. We're in the eye of a new storm. The environment has changed in fundamental ways and won't ever go back to what it was. And we're facing fierce headwinds, the likes of which we have never witnessed before.

I mentioned the industry-wide labor, supply, and drug cost pressures, how government reimbursements fall $100 billion short of actual care costs, and the threat of Medicare insolvency. But there's much more coming our way. We continue to face frightening shortages among clinicians and allied healthcare workers, while chronic disease and the number of elderly Americans is rising. Also, those patients will grow more racially and ethnically diverse, so we will need more and more workers who look like them, as we know outcomes improve when this is the case.

The unprecedented problems we are facing in healthcare require new thinking, bold moves, and solutions that prove how long-held preconceptions about scale are misguided. In the next chapter, I'll share the story of our historic combination of Atrium Health in the Southeast with Advocate Aurora Health in the Midwest, to form the new Advocate Health system. It's part of our answer to creating the next-generation model of what a health system can be into the future. Integrating our two legacy hospital systems provides the financial, technical, and intellectual resources to bring health, hope, and healing to our respective communities, better than they could have been cared for before and in a more cost-effective and affordable way.

Scale, consolidation, merger—these words stir the cauldrons of controversy in the healthcare business perhaps more than in any other industry. But as Ken Kaufman, chair of healthcare management consulting firm Kaufman Hall and arguably the nation's top healthcare expert, notes, the financial morass in which we're entrenched, and the competition hospitals are facing in this new world, point to few other cost-saving options. "Scale," he says, "will help ensure that America's hospitals can keep pace, that they can continue to build on their deep community connections, expertise treating the full range of health conditions, and history of serving our most vulnerable populations."[6]

Most Americans don't think about hospitals until they have chest pain, need a hip replacement, or receive a cancer diagnosis. Notwithstanding the challenges described here, we are your neighbors, brothers, and sisters, dedicated to serving our neighbors, brothers, and sisters.

We show up—for all—no matter what.

CHAPTER 10

Do More, Be Better, Go Faster

The Next Generation Network

I recall from my interview for the CEO position with the search committee that I shared with its members, "This is an organization that has been successful in the past, but I believe the healthcare sector is going to undergo such profound change that what made organizations successful in the past will not necessarily make them successful in the future." In other words, what got you here won't get you there. And if they were to choose me, that would be choosing change.

I wanted to test whether or not ours would be a mutual fit. The search committee chair, Al McAulay, said, "I feel like we have created a jumbo jet that has really served this community well. But while we have landed safely on the tarmac at the airport, we are looking for a new leader to pilot us to a new and better destination." It was his way of saying, "Yes, we are ready to take a leap forward into the unknown future, and we know change is necessary."

So, shortly after I joined the organization in 2016, I invited Carol Lovin, who was then our chief strategy officer, for a visit. "Carol," I said, "the healthcare organization is transforming before our eyes. We are going to need to build new competencies in innovation, education, and clinical expertise . . . while significantly lowering our cost structures. And I believe to do so will require new partnerships and relationships that share the same vision. And we will have to change fast, before we have to."

We decided to call this strategy "Creating the Next Generation Network" (NGN), with the overarching goal to create a new health system with new partners that would be wired together in a way that would become a national model.

Two years later, we changed our name from Carolinas HealthCare System (which was North Carolina–centric) to Atrium Health, to signify that we would be exploring partnerships across state boundaries and that we envisioned a system where many different types of organizations with the same mission could congregate under a common roof, so to speak.

So began our NGN strategy. In 2018, days after changing our name, we announced that Navicent Health in Macon, Georgia, would be joining the family, to better serve communities in central and south Georgia. In 2020, we combined with Wake Forest Baptist Health to create a next-generation academic health system, leading to the expansion of Wake Forest University School of Medicine to a second campus located in The Pearl innovation district in Charlotte. And in the first twenty months after the combination, we had already realized $250 million in cost-out savings—consistent with one of the key goals of the NGN strategy. Then, in 2021, we finalized a strategic combination with Floyd Health, a rural system based in Rome, Georgia, to continue to expand and bring new capabilities, talent, facilities, and technology to serve Georgia and Alabama. Our goal to begin building a national system with high-quality partners was taking shape, and with the savings we achieve, we can continue to invest in communities and do more to tackle inequities.

In addition, there are many essential, behind-the-scenes benefits where scale has led to significantly better care for patients. For example, during a severe shortage of antibiotics that resulted in many hospitals canceling surgeries, Atrium Health had the logistics muscle to secure the drugs and avoid postponing operations, thus also avoiding the added stress it would mean for patients.

Revamping Rural Care Delivery

Access to resources and a vast communications and supply chain infrastructure are some of the advantages that scale brings to the patients we serve. One of the biggest benefits of consolidation to individuals and communities is that care not only remains local but grows with respect to access, including specialty care. And being part of a larger, integrated system is also critical for many struggling rural hospitals.

Take, for example, Anson Community Hospital, at one time an old, crumbling fifty-five-bed facility in Wadesboro, North Carolina. It was losing $8.5 million a year, and the health status of the community was ranked at the very bottom, ninety-five out of 100 North Carolina counties in terms of health. A team of our leaders was assigned the task of partnering with the health department and key stakeholders to reimagine healthcare customized to the needs of that community. Most importantly, they met with grassroots groups to hear directly from them what their needs were. Too often, well-intentioned healthcare leaders decide what is best for the community—and that community, which knows best what they need, can feel left out. The bottom line was that the people living there needed better access to primary care, help with chronic diseases, and behavioral health, rather than fifty-five inpatient beds.

"Lack of access to primary care is the canary in the coal mine," says Scott Reinhardt, our enterprise vice president for network and business development. "If you don't have good primary care, the whole system falls apart."

Why? Because if there is no better option, patients who don't need acute care will flood the emergency department. It is not just the wrong site of care in those instances, it is the more costly one as well.

Many systems might have just closed down the hospital facility. We had no obligation, technically, to stay open there, except for our mission to care *for all*. So rather than close Anson, we rebuilt an innovative acute-care hospital with fewer inpatient beds, one centered on primary care—and what is referred to as a Medical Home model. Now called Atrium Health Anson, the facility offers primary and preventative care on one side of the waiting room and an emergency department on the other side, as well as an operating room, a patient wing, and a core team of providers, telemedicine, and even a helipad for those who need to be transferred, all in one location.

Here is another success story: Wilkes Regional Medical Center in rural North Wilkesboro, North Carolina (pop. 4,239), was just days away from running out of money when our team acquired the struggling hospital and reinvigorated it with capital, strong management, and access to a greater breadth of clinical services. Our goal is to partner with rural communities and providers to develop high-quality systems of care, by shifting the focus from economic survival to healthcare innovation. Today, Atrium Health Wake Forest Baptist/Wilkes Medical Center is an A-rated hospital and is recognized nationally as one of the Top Rural Hospitals by Leapfrog, a nonprofit healthcare watchdog organization. As part of our integrated system, Wilkes Medical Center receives support in fourteen clinical areas, including obstetrics and family medicine, cardiology, and behavioral health, as well as virtual cancer services through Atrium Health Levine Cancer Institute in Charlotte.

Those are just two of many examples that illustrate our strong commitment to improving and sustaining rural care. We are North Carolina's leading provider, treating more than 770,000 North Carolina residents annually at the thirteen rural hospitals we operate; that represents one in four hospital admissions across the state. Providing rural care keeps patients close to home, and our virtual care initiatives will make that even easier to accomplish. Currently, we offer our rural providers a suite of twenty-five virtual care services, including virtual hospital, critical care, specialists, on-demand visits, school-based virtual care, employer clinics, and remote patient monitoring, which total over 300,000 virtual visits annually. We also recognize the critical need for more rural-based doctors, especially primary care providers. To address those shortages, we offer rural-focused residency training programs in and near rural communities, and we are prioritizing a plan to fill the rural provider pipeline through the next-generation Wake Forest University School of Medicine. If it were not for our size and scale, we would simply not be able to focus on rural care, and those communities would struggle.

Our rural care footprint has expanded into Macon and Rome, Georgia, as well as Alabama. In all, Atrium Health serves fifty-seven rural counties across a five-state footprint in the Southeast. Our ability to provide patients with better, faster, more economical service close by is a significant benefit of our large, integrated healthcare platform. And that has been our core motivation for continuing to explore strategic growth combinations, like our latest with Advocate Aurora Health. We have hundreds of proof points on how it benefits the communities we serve.

Going National

On December 2, 2022, Atrium Health combined with Advocate Aurora Heath, a health system operating in Illinois and Wisconsin, making it one of the largest health system consolidations in the United States that year. Advocate Aurora Health has been nationally recognized for its expertise in population health, cardiology, neurosciences, oncology, and pediatrics. It was the twelfth-largest not-for-profit integrated health system in the nation, serving three million patients. It employed nearly 75,000 teammates and contributed approximately $2.5 billion in charitable care and services to its communities annually. Our partnership, now branded Advocate Health, makes us the nation's third-largest nonprofit health system, with more than $27 billion in combined revenues. It is the second-largest health system in the nation with an integrated school of medicine. In all, as Advocate Health, we now serve nearly six million patients, from Chicago and Milwaukee to Charlotte and Winston-Salem.

One question that we received often was "Why combine in the middle of a pandemic?" Our response was that it was the best time to combine, to reinvent the future with another like-minded organization. And, further, in a world of digital and virtual care, geographic distances mattered less and less.

The world of healthcare was changing so rapidly that having the necessary talent, capital structures, and platforms was imperative. We also know that healthcare must be integrated, not disaggregated, to truly meet patients' needs. In 2021, private equity firms invested a record $34.7 billion to acquire healthcare businesses and startups, motivated by the steady growth in demand fueled by the aging population and rise in chronic disease. Leading global companies, Amazon, Microsoft, Apple, Meta, and Alphabet, have entered into the healthcare space. Walgreens, the retail giant, invested $5.2 billion to accelerate its plan to open 600 or more Village Medical practices in its drugstores, to deliver primary, urgent, and specialty care. The commercial payer Cigna Healthcare launched virtual-first primary care health plans with key employers. We saw a boom in outpatient surgery centers, as patient and provider demand grew and Medicare approved reimbursement for more procedures performed at ambulatory surgical centers. Growth-equity investments flowed into companies touting digital health platforms, big data, and machine learning for healthcare applications. All of these companies are significantly larger than us, and while we partner with some, we also needed to have the ability to compete to preserve not-for-profit healthcare.

I remember, when I was growing up, hearing this old pearl of wisdom from my Spanish mother. She would always say, *No postergue hasta mañana lo que puede hacer hoy*—or, in English, Don't put off until tomorrow what you can do today.

It was *our* time to step boldly into a new future (if not us, then who?). So, Atrium Health and Advocate Aurora Health combined around the core belief that we would be much better together in the next decade and beyond—that we could disrupt inequities at their root cause, advance learning and discovery at a time when we had severe clinician shortages, and become the preeminent choice for trusted care wherever our patients were. The pandemic only amplified the factors driving healthcare's evolution, factors like market consolidation and competition, the entrance of private equity into hospital systems, new consumer expectations, workforce shortages, a rapidly advancing digital frontier, a more diverse (and aging) population, and a heightened awareness of health inequities. The speedy development of the COVID-19 vaccine (in just twelve months!) proved how important it is to move quickly in the field of translational research, in implementing new technologies, and in redesigning healthcare services. It helped open our eyes to our critical need to be a world-class learning system and expand our academic platform, to lead in the training of the next generation of clinicians driving innovation.

We believed national challenges required a national system to address. The time was right to help lead in transforming the way care is delivered in the United States—and we could not have found a better partner.

Long before our combination was a gleam in our eyes, Advocate Aurora Health CEO Jim Skogsbergh and I had a strong relationship through our work with the American Hospital Association. We had known each other for over a decade and spent a lot of time together when he was chairman and I was vice chair in 2016, working on many policy issues, such as the regulatory burden on health systems and hospitals, thought leadership on the future of the healthcare workforce, and access to health services in vulnerable rural and urban communities, among others. Jim was someone I had always admired and whom I felt was one of the most forward-looking leaders in the field. He was never satisfied with the status quo. And he personified the Midwestern values of hard work, family, faith, and commitment to community.

I once asked Jim what he wanted his legacy to be. He said, "I don't think in terms of legacy, because then it feels like it's about me. I just want to leave my corner of the world a little better than when I found it."

Most importantly, he was someone I trusted who would keep his word with a handshake. Some mergers break down because of the egos of the leaders, but I knew that would never be an issue with Jim. We had built similar "high-drive, low-ego" cultures. And I couldn't think of a better partner with whom to build a new organization.

A Case for Coming Together

Jim and I first started talking back in 2021. We were at a meeting with top health systems CEOs from around the country when Jim invited me to breakfast the next day. He mentioned that he was planning to retire but that he wanted to lay the foundation for a national system and that we were number one on his and the board's list. He talked about us being co-CEOs for a transitional period before he retired, and he said, "I am proud of the system we built, Gene, and there is no one better I could think of turning the keys over to than you." Given how much I had respected him over the years, I was especially honored. Jim added, "There is one thing, Gene, if we go forward, my board is going to ask a lot of questions about the commitment you guys have toward equity and the elimination of health disparities."

I laughed and said, "Perfect. My board will ask the same questions of you guys!"

That was a telling moment. We had a shared commitment and passion around equity as a shared North Star.

As Jim and I continued our discussions over the following weeks, we grew convinced at how much better our systems could be together as one enterprise. We also knew that some would argue against scale. But we knew from experience that every time we grew we were better equipped to care for patients and community across the spectrum. And we realized that we had many similarities that we intended to build on.

Both organizations had been magnet-designated hospital systems, certified by the American Nurses' Credentialing Center as gold-standard institutions, where nurses were empowered to lead patient care and drive institutional healthcare change and innovations. Advocate Aurora Health and Atrium Health had been called "best places to work" by various organizations and recognized as leaders in diversity, promoting a workforce that reflects the racial and ethnic makeup of the communities we serve.

Both hospital systems have won prestigious awards, for our efforts to integrate diversity and inclusion in all aspects of our healthcare operations. In 2021, the American Hospital Association chose Atrium Health as its recipient of the Carolyn Boone Lewis Equity of Care award, for our work to eliminate health disparities and meet the health, housing, and food needs of our less fortunate neighbors across the Southeast. In 2022, each of Advocate Aurora Health's twenty-seven hospitals earned the LGBTQ+ Healthcare Equality Leader designation from the Human Rights Campaign Foundation, for perfect scores on the Healthcare Equality Index, the nation's foremost survey of healthcare facilities' practices toward equitable treatment of LGBTQ+ patients and employees. This is among the awards that my now co-CEO Jim Skogsbergh is most proud of, because it reaffirmed the ability to provide a safe and inclusive environment where our teams, patients, and communities feel understood and celebrated for who they are.

Ken Kaufman, the healthcare futurist, believes these post-pandemic years provide an opportunity for forward-thinking, operations-oriented, multitasking organizations to grow and come out of the pandemic with a different mindset toward change. In one of his popular blog posts, Ken wrote: "This is a transformative period in American healthcare, when hospital organizations are faced with the need to fundamentally reinvent themselves both financially and clinically."

Our teams identified three key areas where integration would be transformative: clinical excellence and population health management, data analytics to advance research breakthroughs, and consumer-facing digital infrastructure. These three drivers were applied to six pledges we made to our communities: 1. Advance health equity; 2. Improve affordability; 3. Build a next-generation workforce; 4. Elevate clinical preeminence and safety; 5. Accelerate learning and discovery; and 6. Lead environmental sustainability. Our code name during the negotiations was Project Odyssey, because we knew it was going to be a journey of many adventures.

By the time we shed our code name and announced the combination of Atrium Health and Advocate Aurora Health, in the spring of 2022, the climate around hospital mergers had shifted. President Joe Biden issued a sweeping executive order, pushing the Federal Trade Commission (FTC) further to review and revise guidelines for hospital mergers and acquisitions.

Critics of hospital mergers have argued that they create market dominance, limit competition, and drive up healthcare costs, and that therefore all consolidations are bad for consumers.

But those critiques are the opposite of our experience. Every time we have expanded, we have acquired new capabilities and have improved quality and cost structure, through standardizing care, joint purchasing, coordinating patient care, and population health management. The bottom line every time has been that we have been better equipped to care for the needs of our community.

Some critics say that stability can be achieved through partnerships that don't financially bind hospitals together. But loose affiliations rarely result in those benefits. When times are financially challenging—like during and after a global pandemic—legal combinations that integrate culture and resources and spread fixed costs and talent are important to strengthening the fabric of the health delivery network. As for concerns about market power, in most states the dominant insurer has the largest market concentration—not health systems.

While there are examples where a hospital system closes a hospital, these decisions are not made lightly and are largely a function of population shifts to a newer or more popular facility or a result of a population shrinking significantly. What is more common is the dissolution of an affiliation over financial or cultural differences. In fact, early in my career at Atrium Health, we separated a large, well-known practice for those very reasons. Today, I'd like to think we have found a way to coexist, but the separation was disruptive to providers and our patients. The ideal scenario is when two boards of directors, management teams, and teammate populations are culturally and organizationally on the same page. We have that cultural alignment in the combination of Atrium Health and Advocate Aurora Health into Advocate Health. It will ensure the commitment and accountability required to galvanize the changes needed to achieve the cost savings and quality improvements that our patients and communities deserve.

Cultural Alignment Is Essential

Embarking on a hospital merger and integration can be challenging and not for the faint of heart. Consider this: McKinsey research has found that when healthcare organizations combine, they fail to achieve planned synergies 71 percent of the time. Those that *are* successful meet fewer than 50 percent of synergy targets in year one. So, many health systems struggle with strategic combinations for a common reason: they don't combine *completely*.

Analysts report that 70 percent of health systems fail to integrate fully for two main reasons. First, they cling to their own legacy capabilities, which results in duplication and missed cost savings. Instead of focusing on what is best for the whole, the focus is on trying to convince one side to convert to the other way of doing things. And, fundamentally, that is about culture. The ability for teams to speak truth to power, to engage in crucial conversations, to do appreciative inquiry, to be humble—all of this is the soft stuff that becomes the hard stuff in major mergers and combinations. When systems *aren't* culturally aligned along these dimensions, resistance to change is much stronger, and it is much harder to achieve the vision. People hold fast to practiced norms and are less open to accepting new ideas and systems. To quote American author Jim Butcher, it becomes like "oil and water. Orange juice and toothpaste."[1]

But what exactly is "culture"? That's another question we get a lot.

If you think about it, culture is sort of like air. You can't pinch it between two fingers. It's everywhere. And it evolves ever so slightly with every employee who enters or exits the organization. It starts to manifest itself, starts to feel more tangible, the more we work together toward common goals.

I like to think of culture as *the way we do our work*. It's not the initiative itself, but the enabler of all initiatives.

So spending a lot of time on culture from the start is essential. I have found that cultural surveys can sometimes be helpful but not as effective as establishing a set of leadership norms and behaviors from the start.

For example, at the very first meeting we established our top ten guiding principles, which include:

1. Put the interests of the organization first, our partners second, and our own third.
2. Assume virtuous intent.
3. Seek first to understand.
4. Tell it like it is.
5. Create safe space for crucial conversations.
6. Invest in building relationships with each other.
7. Value and honor joint decision-making.
8. Have each other's back.
9. Never let people see daylight between us.
10. Have fun and enjoy the ride together.

Having clearly delineated principles is one thing; living them is where the real magic happens. I credit our ability to hold ourselves accountable to them as key to our success and ability to navigate choppy waters of healthcare in a unified, values-driven way. After all, this is a people business at the core. How the team behaves, I would assert, is even more important than what the strategy is. The "how" matters as much as or more than the "what."

Financial Strength in Service of Community Benefit

One of the things that Jim and I were proud of was that Atrium Health and Advocate Aurora Health were the only not-for-profit hospital systems with AA credit ratings—an Aa3 outlook from Moody's Investors Services and an AA credit rating from S&P Global Ratings—but were among the national leaders in providing community benefit—which is a term defined by the Federal Internal Revenue Code that demonstrates how health systems fulfill their tax-exempt charitable status.

In 2021, for example, the Atrium Health enterprise provided a total of $2.46 billion in measurable community benefits, which broke down like this:

- $375 million cost of care to uninsured and underinsured patients who did not qualify for financial assistance.
- $76 million in cash and in-kind contributions to community health improvement and other community-building activities.
- $227 million to fund professional medical education and research.
- $310 million in losses incurred by serving Medicaid patients.
- $1.1 billion in losses incurred by serving Medicare patients and other non-negotiated government programs.
- $340 million in financial assistance to uninsured and low-income patients, including hardship settlement discounts to patients who have experienced a catastrophic event resulting in large medical bills in excess of $2,500.

As a percentage of operating expense, that $2.4 billion in community benefit was 19.1 percent, greater than the top ten largest health systems in the country.

An important note about that last bullet above. Our financial assistance programs are critically important to residents within Atrium Health's geographic footprint; Medicaid has not been expanded in several of the states we serve, and so we implemented specific policies to expand assistance to those in need and without affordable insurance coverage.

Assistance comes in many forms, depending on the patient's financial needs. For example:

Mary Tanner was a single mother of two with no savings and no health insurance, who earned just $500 per month as a housekeeper. After a very serious and complicated orthopedic surgical procedure, the costs to provide care exceeded $100,000, due to a complicated leg fracture and a five-day inpatient stay. Our financial counselor investigated and determined she would likely qualify for Medicaid and applied on her behalf. The application was approved, and she had no financial responsibility for her bill.

Jeremiah Tucker, a single young adult who worked at a grocery store without health insurance, needed an MRI, at cost of more than $1,000. An automated process determined that, due to his financial situation, his balance would be written off at 100 percent. He never received a bill and didn't have to complete an application.

Rita Owens was a single mother who worked at a fast-food restaurant. She was billed $300 for her teenage son's physical and lab work. An automated process determined that she qualified for financial assistance due to her income level, and her bill was adjusted to a fifty-dollar copay.

Now, combined as Advocate Health, we deliver over $5 billion in charity care and other forms of uncompensated and undercompensated care to uninsured and underserved populations, among other charitable benefits. This makes us one of the leaders among health systems in this regard.

All of these factors and our financial strength, combined with our shared culture to serve the underserved, make the entire enterprise a magnet for recruiting and retaining talent. Our strategic combination enables us to deepen our commitments to health equity, create more jobs and advancement opportunities for our teammates, launch game-changing innovations, and much more, all to elevate the care we provide to every life we touch.

In addition, as a combined entity, the new Advocate Health is ready to do more, be better, and go faster as we strive to become a model non-profit health system for the nation, one that demonstrates how large-scale integration can deliver a life-changing impact on our patients, communities, and teammates. In a rapidly changing healthcare environment, driven by an aging population and lightning-fast digital advances, hospital systems need a bold, even disruptive care model to blaze a new path forward. And Advocate Health is that model. Our ultimate measure of successful integration is "Are our communities healthier because of our combination?"

Our recipe for success is outlined in six pledges, or promises to our communities, that detail exactly what we intend to accomplish by being better together:

1. **Advance Health Equity.** During the first five years of our life as a combined healthcare system, Advocate Health is investing $2 billion to disrupt the root causes of health inequities.

   How we'll do it: As a large, integrated system, we are already a vast research engine focused on health equity, with established clinical programs for underserved populations, such as the South Asian Cardiovascular Center, Adult Down Syndrome Center, and Hypertension and Diabetes Programs for Black and Latino/a communities. During the crisis in war-torn Syria more than six years ago, Atrium Health East Charlotte Family Physicians established a refugee services group to care for an influx of new patients.

   Access continues to be a barrier to equitable healthcare in urban and rural communities, so we are building new local care centers and growing our virtual healthcare initiatives and well-being services. Rural hospitals pose a unique set of problems because of their remoteness, aging facilities, and difficulty retaining doctors and nurses. According to the American Hospital Association, more than 100 rural hospitals have closed since 2010. The examples of Anson Community Hospital and Wilkes Regional Medical Center, which I gave earlier in this chapter, are just a few of the ways we're bolstering our commitment to rural populations. More recently, we've developed a cross-functional team of Atrium Health rural experts called the SEAL Team, which stands for Spot issues, Evaluate, take Action for Lasting results. This group of clinicians and administrators can be deployed for e-consults, to supplement primary care, and to close the specialty care gap wherever and whenever needed in our enterprise's footprint.

   Our success with identifying neighborhoods in need of masks and COVID-19 vaccines during the pandemic taught us the power of comprehensive, up-to-date databases and digital monitoring systems. So, we are doubling down on the use of digital dashboards that can pinpoint health equity gaps at the neighborhood and street level, so we can quickly deploy tailored interventions.

Another way Advocate Health will disrupt health inequities is by addressing social determinants of health, such as hunger, homelessness, employment, and literacy. These are areas that traditionally have not been in the scope of influence of hospitals and health systems but must be a part of our mission as we move into the future. Working with local governments, businesses, and community partners, we will invest in our communities, through advancing programs for such things as safe, affordable housing, food security, violence prevention, and stable employment. And we've committed an annual spend of over $500 million to help minority- and women-owned businesses to grow, including minority- and women-owned vendors and suppliers to our clinics and hospitals. With such a robust catalog of efforts to intentionally close the gaps that prevent equitable service, experience, and outcomes, we believe the Advocate National Center for Health Equity we are building in Milwaukee, Wisconsin can serve as a catalyst for progress across the country. As one of the largest providers in the nation for bringing health, hope, and healing to Medicaid recipients and other vulnerable, underserved populations, Advocate Health will have a seat at the table, to influence healthcare reforms at the national level.

2. **Improve Affordability.** There is no denying that healthcare must become more affordable and that all players in the sector must play a role. The average premium for family coverage has increased 20 percent over the last five years and 43 percent over the last ten years, according to recent statistics from the American Hospital Association. People are worried, and families are making decisions between healthcare and other important priorities, such as food, transportation, and other critical needs.

How we'll do it: Combining the healthcare entities into one large enterprise, one team of teams with a suite of enterprise-shared services, is already resulting in substantial savings in fixed costs associated with the supply chain through group purchasing, information technology, back-office overhead, and pharmacy and laboratory operations, among others. Standardizing clinical procedures drives savings, which we reinvest, leading to quality improvements and innovation. All of these benefits and cost savings allow integrated systems like ours to improve care and lower the cost to patients.

One highly transparent way to demonstrate the cost-saving benefits of scale to individuals is through our deep commitment to extending care to the most vulnerable patients via our expanded Charity Care policies, which are among the most generous in the country. Specifically, we guarantee that anyone who is at or below 300 percent of the Federal Poverty Level receives free care across all of the communities we serve. So a family of four making less than $60,000 would have free access. To that point, Atrium Health absorbed $1,438,075,643 in losses serving Medicare and Medicaid patients in 2021.

Furthermore, as one system, Advocate Health is a national leader in value-based care, with 2.2 million of our patients participating in a health delivery model where we are incentivized to improve health quality and outcomes and decrease costs. Through these new models, we have saved the government and patients over $500 million in costs—and achieved top-quality scores. Together we are expanding access for our most vulnerable patients by shifting care to low-cost virtual and digital options.

On the horizon: We plan to conduct research into novel, value-based care programs, by establishing a Center for Applied Research for the Advancement of Value-Based Care, to share our learnings nationally on how to continue to improve quality and decrease costs.

3. **Build Next-Generation Workforce.** Through our continued growth, investment, and innovation, Advocate Health is positioning itself to be a model for the future of medical education, while increasing the number and diversity of healthcare professionals and widening the pipeline of medical

professionals at all levels who will serve rural and underserved urban areas. Our new, second, state-of-the-art Wake Forest University School of Medicine, in The Pearl innovation district in Charlotte, will fuel that pipeline by educating more than 3,500 total healthcare learners, including nursing and medical students, residents, and fellows across more than 100 specialized training programs annually. Many from this new crop of talent will find careers at Advocate Health. But our system will also be a magnet for talented teammates who don't have advanced degrees. We estimate creating more than 20,000 new jobs over the next ten years. At the same time, we'll enable career advancement of our current teammates at every level and train the next generation of clinicians in the most innovative practices. The results will be greater work flexibility for our workforce, a supportive and inclusive work environment, better wages across our footprint, and advancement opportunities that will yield leaders who reflect the communities we serve.

How we'll do it: We've been recognized by *Forbes* magazine as among the "Best Employers by State" in Illinois, North Carolina, South Carolina, and Wisconsin. And we'll continue to make our combined system a great place to work through culture-building initiatives, career development programs, and commitment to a living wage across our footprint. During the pandemic, for example, we earmarked more than $600 million for minimum wage increases and other market adjustments. Further, we are using artificial intelligence to redefine the nature of work and put the best tools in the hands of our clinicians, while decreasing the hassle factor. Additionally, with our focus on inclusion and priorities like environmental sustainability, we are attracting bright new minds to help us reinvent healthcare delivery and take on newly created roles.

4. **Elevate Clinical Preeminence and Safety.** First and foremost, our overarching goal is to be the highest-quality and safest clinical enterprise that is also the most trusted choice for care, and we pledged to be in top decile performance for health

outcomes. For one, by coming together we are better equipped to meet the challenges of an aging population. By 2035, one in five U.S. residents will be over the age of sixty-five. Our nation's health systems need to prepare today to help this important population achieve a better quality of life as they age. As Advocate Health, we have been able to attract the top national talent to help with aging and have one of the top dementia and Alzheimer's programs in the nation. We believe we can make a significant difference by improving the lives of our seniors, for example, over this next decade.

How we'll do it: As a large, collaborative entity, Advocate Health is also advancing large, multisite, patient-centered research to combat metabolic diseases like diabetes, hypertension, heart and vascular disease, and other disorders that affect millions of Americans. Much of that research work is being done in the innovation corridor between Winston-Salem's Innovation Quarter and Charlotte's innovation district, The Pearl. It is quickly becoming a nationally recognized space for health innovation, where physicians, inventors, scientists, and other visionaries collaborate on bleeding-edge technologies and treatments. In years to come, that science work will yield groundbreaking advances in precision medicine, screening, early diagnosis, and treatment, which will greatly improve outcomes. What's more, our advanced data and analytics capability, along with machine learning, will inform how we practice virtual medicine in the future, an area where we are already a national leader with nearly two million annual visits.

5. **Accelerate Learning and Discovery.** I mentioned the goal to become the Silicon Valley of health innovation. We are well on our way, with the partnership with IRCAD and the North American research and training headquarters at The Pearl in Charlotte and the well-established Wake Forest Institute of Regenerative Medicine in Winston-Salem, where scientists are engineering replacement tissues to remedy the shortages in donor organs, for example. Also, Advocate Health is becoming one of the nation's leading educators of new physicians, with

2,000 residents and fellows in 172 residency programs and two Wake Forest University Medical School campuses, in Winston-Salem and Charlotte. By promoting research and learning across our footprint, we'll be able to bring advanced diagnostics and treatments to the bedside. Powered by AI, robotics, virtual reality, and other technology advancements, we'll be able to build a world-class experiential learning platform to train best-in-class clinicians. Our work in integrating genomics and epigenetics through precision medicine has the potential to increase our understanding of the origins of disease and improve public health and health equity.

How we'll do it: Within five years, Advocate Health will have among the largest (and actionable) provider-based research data sets in the country, with thirty-seven million unique patient records. That vast resource gives us the opportunity to fuel a robust research engine, funded by hundreds of millions in research grants that we receive every year. We will also have one common Institute Review Board—which is an independent review board to oversee our research trials—and also to reach out and build trust in minority populations, to enroll them in clinical trials. In other words, the goal is to be a trusted voice in the face of the horrible legacy of the Tuskegee experiments on Black Americans.

6. **Lead Environmental Sustainability.** Our goal is to achieve carbon neutrality by 2030 and strive for net-zero carbon by 2035, to protect the earth for future generations. Committing to being an environmentally responsible organization is not only beneficial to our earth; implementing sustainable and ethical practices scratches our own backs, too. It lowers operational costs, with benefits including lower utility bills. It elevates the positive image of our brand and builds greater trust among patients and our communities. And it results in teammates who feel good about working here, which improves retention. Most important of all, creating an environmentally sustainable healthcare system is another way hospital systems improve public health. Eliminating poor practices that create waste and pollution and contribute

to resource exhaustion makes for healthier, more resilient communities. And the institutional efficiencies that effort results in allow us to divert dollars saved to better patient care.

How we'll do it: It takes an enterprise-wide effort every day to reduce energy use and waste through practices that reduce the use of plastics, paper, and harmful chemicals. Our plans include increasing energy efficiency in all our facilities and, especially, focusing on the new facilities we are building. We recently opened an LEED silver hospital in Wisconsin and are building the first net-zero-carbon medical school in the nation. We've also grown our fleet of electric vehicles. And we are incentivizing our teammates, through discounts in their benefit payments, to become more energy-conscious at home. We were an ENERGY STAR Partner of the Year in 2018 and 2019 and a Partner of the Year— Sustained Excellence in 2020, 2021, and 2022. Atrium Health is one of only two health systems to receive this highly coveted designation for two or more consecutive years. We intend to build on those efforts.

We've already made significant progress to date. Going forward, we will also measure success through tons of waste diverted from landfills through enterprise-wide recycling efforts and supply chain sustainable sourcing.

* * *

These pledges are our road map for the future. They are our commitment to improving every community we serve. And we intend to hold ourselves accountable to them.

Final Observations and Lessons Learned

I was recently asked by a group of healthcare CEOs what were the key lessons I had learned in growing our system. I have compiled them here:

- The guiding question and number one measure of success should be: Are our **communities better** than before we came together?

- **Cultures must be compatible:** Choose partners who have similarly high-drive and low-ego cultures. This influences both the compatibility of the leadership teams and the long-term ability to create value for communities.
- **Doing deals can require a leap of faith:** The process of negotiating a deal can tell you a lot about what it's like to work with a partner. That is where you can have the first real glimpse into cultural compatibility.
- **Best-in-class integration capabilities are nonnegotiable:** A five-year journey to value for communities is too long. In integration, Advocate Health has taken a deliberate middle path that balances system-ness with ensuring appropriate local decision-making, as going too far to one extreme or the other can be problematic. It's important to remember that small integrations can be as much work as large integrations.
- **Never forget who is on the front line and who is supporting:** It is important to protect the ability of the front line to continue to serve patients throughout the deal and integration process.

Governance and board culture are of paramount importance as well. Set the guiding behavioral principles early.

We will continue to draw on these lessons in future combinations, to ensure we continue to grow in a way that is consistent with our mission and vision for healthcare in America.

CHAPTER 11

Eight Prescriptions for the Future of Healthcare *For All*

At a time of divided politics, there is one thing most of us can agree on: we are at a pivotal moment in the healthcare sector, and as a nation. The pandemic has proven that we can accomplish amazing feats in the face of extreme adversity. It is time to draw on those lessons and experiences for the road ahead. At Atrium Health and Advocate Aurora Health, we tackled the pandemic just as we would care for a patient in our intensive-care unit: by working as a team, leveraging technology, bringing the best practices to bear, and—most importantly—never giving up on our patients.

The sobering truth of the matter is that our entire healthcare system is ailing and in intensive care. How do we fix it? How do we create a system that makes people truly healthier while significantly reducing costs? There have been many efforts to try to do so, but it is among the greatest challenges we face in this country. What's more, the challenge is also a national security risk. More than 30 percent of young Americans are disqualified for the military service due to obesity, according to a study by the Council for a Strong America called "Unhealthy and Unprepared." This is but one example among thousands for why a profound shift is required. The ramifications for failing to reinvent our health system are broad and profound. We are at the proverbial tipping point.

As I stated at the beginning of this book, I set out to tell the story of how our healthcare heroes battled through the pandemic, from my vantage point as a CEO committed to caring for his troops. I also wanted to show readers how healthcare operates under the hood and where and how the healthcare sector has broken down, while offering real, evidence-based solutions that can make a real, significant impact. It won't be easy, and we'll need to play the long game, but our nation, and its viability into the future, is counting on us.

In light of that, here are my top eight prescriptions to help heal our country's health sector:

PRESCRIPTION ONE

Double the investment in public health with a focus on chronic disease

As Benjamin Franklin put it, "An ounce of prevention is worth a pound of cure."

But that's not how healthcare works in the United States. We typically wait until symptoms send us to our doctors or to an emergency department. We get a diagnosis and then we're treated with pricey drugs and expensive surgeries. Nonetheless, we continue to cut funding until a public health crisis, like a pandemic, delivers a wake-up call.

It's a reactionary system. Intervening after the fact can be more difficult than preventing the disease, disorder, or public health crisis in the first place, and it often multiplies the cost.

Take, for example, a pervasive health threat like heart disease. The number one cause of heart disease (and stroke) is high blood pressure, because it damages the lining of the arteries, making them less flexible and more susceptible to a buildup of plaque. This narrows the arteries, cutting off blood flow to the heart and brain.

Hypertension is treatable and preventable. It can be avoided or lowered by eating healthier foods, losing weight, exercising, stopping smoking, and limiting alcohol consumption, in addition to medication. And yet three in four of the 116 million U.S. adults with high blood pressure don't have it under control. The consequences of uncontrolled hypertension—heart disease and stroke—are among the nation's leading causes of death and disability, racking up $321 billion each year in direct medical costs and lost productivity.

Additionally, nearly half of all Americans over the age of fifty-four suffer from two or more chronic disorders, such as diabetes, chronic obstructive pulmonary disease (COPD), cardiovascular disease, and cancer, each one very expensive to manage and treat. But what if we could put more public funds toward supporting better nutrition, access to exercise, and preventative testing? What if we could make blood pressure screening easier and more accessible to those who are unaware they have hypertension and then help them take proactive steps? The Centers for Disease Control and Prevention says reducing the number of people with high blood pressure alone could save billions in healthcare costs yearly. It estimates that a team-based intervention involving community health workers, social workers, and health professionals, such as nurses and pharmacists, could prevent up to 91,900 heart attacks, 139,000 strokes, and 115,400 cardiovascular deaths over five years, saving Medicare up to $900 million. Simply reducing the population's average sodium consumption to the recommended maximum 2,300 mg a day could reduce high blood pressure cases by eleven million annually, saving $18 billion in healthcare costs.[1] And that's just by reducing hypertension. What about the obesity and type 2 diabetes epidemics in our country? At our current rates of overweight and metabolic disorders, one in every three children in the United States will develop type 2 diabetes in their lifetimes.

Doubling the approximately $100 billion we currently invest in public health and human services to prevent chronic disease could be among the most economically sound moves we can make. Studies show that every dollar invested in public health yields improved health outcomes equivalent to eighty-eight dollars in expenditures saved by county public health departments. Even if we achieve only 50 percent of that return, we more than justify the extra investment.

Additionally, we must operate the public health system more cohesively and efficiently, partnering effectively with other stakeholders like health systems and ensuring information flows seamlessly. Currently, the U.S. public health system is a mishmash of federal, state, and local agencies and departments. During the pandemic, in most communities around the nation, many local health departments operated independently, reinventing the wheel more times than not. We need a new organizing paradigm that unifies efforts, efficiently disseminates best practices, and standardizes and consolidates back-office functions. These steps could save hundreds of millions of dollars—just as we have achieved at our health system by implementing these efficiencies. This will help ensure that additional funds invested in public health actually deliver on improving health outcomes, versus having them squandered in bureaucracy.

Related to this, we must further invest in a well-trained public health workforce that is resourced in rural areas and low-income communities, where it's most needed. Federal and state policymakers should create new incentives, like bonuses, loan repayment, and career growth incentives, to recruit and retain frontline public health workers. Additionally, to better target communities in need, we should have a comprehensive data system that updates in real time and "hot spots" communities disproportionately affected by health issues, so that resources and interventions can be deployed to close the gaps in access and care. Our public health information system is antiquated and uncoordinated. This was particularly evident during the pandemic, when systems like ours had to rely on our own data scientists to hotspot communities in need. Unfortunately, most smaller health systems do not have that capability.

The bottom line is that, from premature deaths to a heavier disease burden, the United States ranks behind most other industrialized nations. Hospital-related admissions for diabetes and congestive heart failure, for example, are higher in the United States than in most comparable countries.

Doubling the size of our investment in public health can begin to reverse the tide and reduce the disease burden that shows up in our hospital emergency rooms—where costs can be highest and some diseases are caught too late.

PRESCRIPTION TWO

Make telehealth and home-based programs permanent
Althea sat on the edge of her hospital bed, smiling at her husband, John. She was happy to be going home. The seventy-seven-year-old had been

admitted two days prior for a rapid heartbeat and swelling in her legs. Her COPD, which made it difficult to breathe, had put additional strain on her heart, and she had developed congestive heart failure.

Althea's doctors said she could go home if she agreed to participate in Atrium Health's Hospital at Home Program. She jumped at the chance to be home, in a familiar place, with her family.

Atrium Health Hospital at Home is available to patients who need hospital-level care but not intensive care. We developed the program during the pandemic, to address the short supply of hospital beds—and we ended up becoming one of the largest providers of hospital at home in the entire nation.

Althea went home with a small device attached to her upper arm, which sent her heart rate, respirations, blood oxygen levels, and temperature readings to a 24/7 virtual nursing team. She also received a tablet that provided her with a direct audio/video connection to her nurse 24/7, in case she had a question or needed help. Althea received two in-home visits per day from a community paramedic, who administered an intravenous diuretic to reduce excess fluid caused by heart failure. She also had a daily virtual visit with her physician. She was getting excellent care, in the comfort of her own home.

Out of necessity, virtual healthcare has seen record growth since the early days of COVID-19. According to research from the National Institutes of Health, 88 percent of patients believe that virtual visits with physicians were more convenient than in-person appointments, and 85 percent found them to be as reliable as in-person visits. Nearly 98 percent of surveyed patients said they were satisfied with their telemedicine visits. Preliminary data also shows that quality outcomes were on par with hospital care.

In addition, the impact of telemedicine has already been felt powerfully in rural settings, where in-person access to clinicians and hospitals is often limited. According to the Centers for Disease Control and Prevention, rural residents are more likely to die from chronic diseases than their urban or suburban-living counterparts. Why? One key reason is lack of access to providers and clinics, medical technology, and specialists, including behavioral health expertise. Often, rural residents must drive long distances to reach major hospitals or university medical centers that offer the specialized care they need. We have used our tele-health platform to effectively meet the needs of the most rural communities we serve, from connecting patients with a behavioral health specialist, to beaming in an infectious disease physician to a rural hospital during COVID-19, because the hospital simply wouldn't have that expertise on-site.

Telehealth eliminates barriers

The costs versus benefits of telehealth have been debated for decades. But the pandemic proved without a doubt how efficient telehealth could be. It provides an easy way for people to access care wherever they happen to be, through a device that's already in their pocket or on a desk in their home.

Consider a review of nine randomized clinical trial studies, involving 959 adult patients with a chronic disease, that compared hospital-at-home interventions to in-hospital stays. The paper published online in 2021 by the *Journal of the American Medical Association*[2] found that although patients receiving hospital at home care spent about five days longer recovering, they had a 26 percent lower risk of readmission and a lower risk of long-term care admission, relative to the in-hospital group. Preventing readmission translates to dollars saved and peace of mind for patients. In addition, hospital at home patients reported fewer symptoms of depression and anxiety, compared to patients receiving in-hospital care. Also, the likelihood of developing a hospital-borne infection, like staph or MRSA, was reduced.

As we face a looming crisis—an aging population—hospitals are not prepared for the numbers. The Centers for Disease Control and Prevention reports that we're 15,000 beds short of what are currently needed to care for our population, and that's not even counting our old hospital infrastructure that's in need of replacement.

Our experience with virtual care suggests that if we adopt it broadly, the United States can bridge the gap and specifically:

- Reduce hospital overcrowding
- Reduce the number of net inpatient beds over time
- Improve outcomes
- Reduce clinician and staff burnout

- Relieve patient stress and anxiety

Telehealth can also reduce barriers to access for low-income individuals who might lack insurance, transportation, or childcare or who can't take off work without losing wages. To do that effectively, it is important to note that we must simultaneously bridge the digital divide that disproportionally impacts rural and challenged urban communities.

The "doctor's office" in school

There are incredible proof points for telehealth and evidence of its transformational impact on patients and communities. In Peach County, in central Georgia, we've seen this impact firsthand. Peach County is a rural area with a diverse population and a small school district. Access to healthcare is one of the biggest hurdles parents living in this area face. When a child becomes ill at school, it often means the parent must leave work and shuttle their child from school to a doctor's office or, if they don't have a primary care physician, to the emergency department at Atrium Health Navicent Peach Medical Center. The disruption could take most of the day.

To help keep parents at work and students in school, the Peach County School District partnered with Atrium Health Navicent to implement a school-based virtual healthcare program for students, teachers, and school staff that was based on our similar programs in school districts in the Charlotte region. Here's how the system works: if the school nurse determines that a child needs to be seen by a doctor, the nurse will call the parent or guardian for permission to initiate a virtual medicine session. Next, the nurse contacts a remotely located Navicent primary care doctor, who sends one of the medical assistants/telepresenters assigned to the school to the nurse's office, to facilitate the telemedicine visit with the provider. The parent can attend the virtual visit through a smartphone. Using a device with a high-definition camera, the medical assistant conducts a physical exam, allowing the doctor to peer into the student's ears, nose, and throat, as well as listen to breathing and heart sounds. Most of the ailments are typical problems that affect kids: cold and flu-like symptoms, pink eye, lice, and ear infections. In many cases, students can return to class while the provider calls in a prescription to a local pharmacy, and the parent doesn't have to leave work.

So far, the program is a tremendous success. During the first year of service at six Peach County schools, through Navicent Peach Medical Center, 62 percent of visits resulted in students being returned to class, demonstrating that the virtual care program has been able to reduce early dismissal from school and reduce disruptions to student and parents. System-wide, Atrium Health's school-based virtual health programs have led to an approximately 30 percent reduction in emergency department visits among students served.

The evidence for virtual care and hospital at home care is clear, from a provider's as well as a patient's perspective—but it has to make financial sense for hospitals and providers to become a permanent part of the menu of options for patients. In the federally declared public health emergency, during the pandemic, hospitals were able to apply for waivers that would reimburse at-home care at the same rates as in-person care. This must become a permanent part of how we treat patients, remove barriers to care and prevent disease—not just during a pandemic. To take away this offering would be a setback for rural communities, working parents, seniors, and more.

PRESCRIPTION THREE

Dramatically reduce drug costs through adopting a negotiating model similar to that used by the U.S. Department of Veterans Affairs

If there is one thing Americans in this politically divided nation can agree upon, it's that prices are simply too high. Americans spend more on prescription drugs per capita than citizens in any other industrialized country in the world. But let's put those exorbitant price tags on the shelf for a moment and recognize that we in the United States are the beneficiaries of a level of biopharmaceutical innovation that's unmatched anywhere. Big and small pharma here deliver 57 percent of all new medications that treat patients throughout the world. In recent years, talented scientists at U.S.-based companies have developed breakthrough, life-altering treatments for heart disease, diabetes, cancer, kidney disease, and even Alzheimer's disease, bringing hope and healing to millions of individuals and families. And the recent creation of a COVID-19 vaccine within one year is as remarkable a feat as we have seen in humankind, a feat that saved millions of lives.

We are fortunate to have these treatments available, but they come at a steep price. The question is, "Does the price have to be *that* steep?"

Preserve the 340B Program to Combat Rising Drug Costs

Recognizing how expensive drug acquisition is for providers, Congress created the 340B drug discount program, which requires drug manufacturers to sell outpatient drugs at a discount to safety-net providers serving high numbers of low-income Medicare, Medicaid, and Supplemental Security Insurance patients. The congressional intent of the program is to allow these providers to "stretch scarce federal resources as far as possible, reaching more eligible patients and providing more comprehensive services." Savings from the program help fund free and low-cost medications in our qualifying facilities, but this is one of the only tools at our disposal to combat rising drug costs within our system, and we use the savings to offer a wide array of expanded services to benefit the communities we serve. We must continue to protect this program, to be able to meet the needs of our patients.

You may have heard this statistic: It takes about ten years and \$1 billion to \$3 billion on average to invent and bring just one new drug to market. The pharmaceutical industry argues that high drug prices are necessary to recoup that massive investment in research and development—which seems reasonable. But is it true?

In 2022, a study published online in *JAMA Network Open* by a team of economics researchers made news by answering, "No."[3] R&D costs do not explain the high drug price increases in the United States in recent years. In fact, another study by America's Health Insurance Plans (AHIP) found that drug manufacturers often spend more on sales and marketing than on research and development for new cures and medical treatments.

Additionally, rules requiring prior authorizations and "fail first" or "step therapy" policies, which require patients to fail on the insurer's preferred drug before they can take the drug originally prescribed, create high barriers to more effective medications and add to lost time receiving proper treatment. Some studies suggest that patients from communities of color and those with chronic diseases, such as autoimmune diseases and diabetes, are more likely to face these health plan barriers than other Americans who take prescription drugs.

Drug pricing is determined by a complex web of factors and influences, including individual insurance coverage, inflation in the cost of drugs, assessments of effectiveness in payment policies, and medical practice reimbursements, among others. Any solution to making drugs more affordable will not come easily, as we've seen through stalemates on this issue in Congress. But we must continue to advance the ball as prices continue to rise.

In the summer of 2022, President Joe Biden signed into law the Inflation Reduction Act of 2022, which had strong bipartisan support and lowered prescription drug costs for people on Medicare. In the twelve months before the law was signed, there were 1,216 pharmaceuticals whose price increases averaged 31.6 percent, far exceeding the inflation rate of 8.5 percent for that period. The new act requires drugmakers to pay rebates for drugs in Medicare whose price increases exceed inflation. Another key provision of the Inflation Reduction Act allows the Secretary of Health and Human Services to negotiate prices for some popular prescription medications. The legislation may face legal challenges, but it's a step in the right direction. But why not negotiate *all* drugs?

Like many have argued, I say let's draw from the lessons learned by the U.S. Department of Veterans Affairs (VA), which has realized sizable savings in drug costs for its large veteran population. The VA and Medicare are the largest purchasers of pharmaceuticals in the United States, covering prescription drugs for more than fifty-two million people. But the programs are quite different, especially in how they pay for drugs. Medicare reimburses plan sponsors who in turn pay the pharmacies for the medications, while the VA buys drugs directly from pharmaceutical manufacturers. Medicare's beneficiaries have dozens of prescription drug plans, each of which separately negotiates drug prices with manufacturers. The VA is a single integrated health system that negotiates one price for each drug on a master list of covered drugs and medical supplies, called the National Formulary.

Originally, the VA operated under a decentralized system, like Medicare, and was unable to take advantage of its potential bargaining power with drug companies, particularly for classes of medications commonly used by veterans. Then, in 1997, the VA consolidated drug purchases into a single National Formulary. Bulk orders of preferred drugs and blanket purchase agreements with pharmaceutical manufacturers enabled the VA to be more aggressive in negotiating drug prices, resulting in substantial savings. In a recent Government Accounting Office (GAO) study that sampled 399 brand name and generic prescription drugs, the VA paid an average of 54 percent less per unit than Medicare. The GAO found that 233 of those drugs were 50 percent cheaper than in Medicare, and 106 were at least 75 percent cheaper.

In addition, pharmacy benefit managers are one actor in a complicated web that influences the price of drugs. One other avenue to pursue is simplifying the system by reducing the number of different players who stand between a patient, a physician, and the company manufacturing the drug the patient needs.

It is clear that ways to bring down prices of prescription drugs can be found. We need an honest discussion among all players to rein in costs. And time is of the essence. Almost one in three Americans have stopped taking a prescription medicine due to the high price, according to Kaiser Family Foundation polling. They're making the tough choice between buying medicine and buying food and paying heating bills.

Why do we fail to realize that when people with chronic diseases don't take their medicine, they can become ill and end up in the hospital? Consider just one example: a diabetic who can't afford insulin may end up needing a leg amputated, at a cost of nearly $80,000 and untold physical, emotional, and financial suffering. Or they may die.

PRESCRIPTION FOUR

Stop insurance companies from making patients and providers jump through hoops with burdensome administrative policies such as prior authorizations
George W., a retired postal worker and avid golfer, spent five days in one of our hospitals recovering from a stroke. He couldn't walk. He struggled

to feed himself. His doctors decided that he needed to be moved to an acute stroke rehab facility. His wife, May, notified the insurance company. After an hour of bouncing between four insurance representatives, she was told their plan wouldn't cover the special rehab. It was medically unnecessary, they said, because her husband didn't have a spinal cord injury.

George's case is like thousands across the country. Insurers create inaccurate or overly rigorous medical necessity policies that deny patients the care their physicians recommend.

"We were seeing denials for medically necessary, inpatient rehabilitation care for people who suffered a significant stroke or spinal cord injury—people who would very easily qualify under any reasonable interpretation of the coverage criteria," says Brian Moore, MD, Atrium Health's chief medical officer for physician advisor services.

When Dr. Moore met George and his wife, George was sobbing: "I paid into this plan all my life and I thought I was protected."

Dr. Moore called the insurance plan. He was told he would need to file another application for approval, a process that could take three to five days. He made more calls, was transferred a half-dozen times, and finally reached someone who rattled off incomprehensible regulations. The rep asked him, "What's your ICD10 diagnosis? Was there a medicine to prevent the need for stroke rehab?"

"I've been doing this for years and years and it was fatiguing to *me*," says Dr. Moore. "Imagine how a patient feels while also dealing with the physical and emotional trauma of a serious illness."

It took a week and pages of faxed medical records and other documents to appeal the denial before George's acute rehab was finally approved. Too long, says Dr. Moore. "Your ability to improve your function after a stroke is dependent upon how quickly you receive the kind of intense rehab you only get in a stroke facility."

Prior authorization hassles and denials create dangerous delays in care and often lead to patients abandoning treatment, according to a 2021 survey of physicians by the American Medical Association. They're also a burden to providers (doctors often report spending two full workdays weekly on preauthorization paperwork) and exponentially drive up administrative costs for the healthcare system. A 2019 survey of hospitals by the American Hospital Association revealed that one large national health system spends $15 million per month on administrative costs associated with insurer prior authorization changes.

We need to enact reforms that prevent insurance companies from unnecessarily impeding access to care, which actually drives up costs through policies and procedures that cause delays, denials, and hoops for patients and providers to jump through. Also, the rules governing approvals and payments must be simplified and standardized across plans, so that the insurance administrators themselves can understand how to apply them appropriately. Some studies have shown that, for example, 75 percent of prior authorizations and payment denials are overturned when beneficiaries and providers appeal. That means the plans initially got it wrong, and as a result patients lost crucial time receiving the treatments that hospitals and their doctors ordered.

If we want to make the U.S. healthcare system more affordable to all, we must tackle this head-on, along with the unnecessary burden on our healthcare workforce. Policymakers and insurance commissioners have a responsibility to stop insurers from hassling providers and their patients.

PRESCRIPTION FIVE

Invest in growing the next generation of clinicians to address severe workforce shortages

Physicians, nurses, and allied health professionals such as cardio technologists, diagnostic medical sonographers, physician's assistants, anesthesiologist assistants, occupational therapists, and others, form the backbone of the U.S. healthcare industry. But we don't have enough people in these roles right now, and projections suggest the situation will become even more challenging. For instance, the Association of American Medical Colleges projects that by 2033 the United States will be short 124,000 physicians.

If we don't address the shortages of these essential workers, we will see poorer patient outcomes. There will be more falls, hospital-acquired infections, medical mistakes, and increased chances of death, according to the American Association of Colleges of Nursing. Shortages also hit rural communities especially hard and worsen health equity gaps.

The United States is not the only country to suffer from a staffing shortage of healthcare workers. The World Health Organization predicts a shortfall of fifteen million healthcare workers worldwide in 2030. The International Centre on Nurse Migration projects a shortage of thirteen million nurses alone by 2030, up from a shortage of six million before the pandemic.

The long-term solution cannot be to recruit help from countries that are themselves in desperate need. The higher education system in the United States must ramp up to meet our domestic need. But to address the shortage of doctors, nurses, and allied health workers, we need more qualified educators to teach them. The retirements of aging instructors and the low pay for educators to replace them has severely reduced the number of programs available to students. We are turning away promising students—including more than 70,000 qualified applicants yearly from nursing programs—because we don't have the faculty capacity. And it is not limited to nursing. The Association of American Medical Colleges has sounded the alarm that, while medical school enrollment continues to grow, there are not enough residency programs and clinical training sites for students to complete their training.

Hospitals, higher education, the private sector, and state and federal governments must work together to increase the pool of faculty and training sites, while developing long-term strategies to repair the holes in the pipeline of healthcare professionals. That effort must include recruiting more people of color and others from marginalized communities into the healthcare professions, which will ultimately improve quality of care for those communities.

There are also tools available to tackle shortages much sooner, especially for people who live in rural and remote places that are considered HPSAs, or Health Professional Shortage Areas. Encourage state lawmakers to allow clinicians to operate at the top of their licenses and across state lines through a national compact agreement. "Operating at the top of license" means the clinician does the work to the full extent they were trained and educated to do, instead of doing tasks that could be done by someone with lesser training and authority. For example, most states currently require nurse practitioners to practice only under the authority of a physician. As such, nurse practitioners aren't being used to the best of their abilities and often end up doing the work a nurse could do. In turn, a nurse might be relegated to doing the work of a nurse's aide or medical assistant. Allowing practitioners to work at the top of licensure would result in greater efficiency, more patients being seen, less physician burnout, cost savings, and better overall care.

Finally, part of what is factoring into the physician shortage is an overemphasis on training physicians in specialties while under-emphasizing the critical field of primary care. We can and should incentivize the practice of primary care through a completely revised reimbursement system, to improve access to primary care physicians and allied health professionals in historically marginalized (including disadvantaged urban and rural) communities. Every option should be on the table, from low-interest loans with minimal penalty fees for those pursuing primary care, to investing in the National Health Service Corps, to expanding the number of primary care residency program slots and narrowing the compensation gap between primary and specialty care.

PRESCRIPTION SIX

Reimagine and fully fund behavioral healthcare

One in five adults experience mental illness in any given year in the United States, according to the CDC. More than 24 percent of adults with mental illness report an unmet need for treatment. More than 2.5 million youth in the United States suffer severe major depression; 14.5 percent of them are youth who identify as more than one race. The pandemic exacerbated the problem, while gaps in our public health and social service infrastructure made a bad situation even worse.

Mental health conditions range in severity from depression and anx-iety disorders to post-traumatic stress disorder, borderline personality disorder, and schizophrenia and include substance use disorders and sui-cidal ideation. And, like most health issues, mental illness disproportion-ately impacts people of color, low-income people, and those experiencing homelessness.

Our nation is in the midst of a mental health care crisis. Behavioral healthcare has been underfunded and stigmatized for far too long. We lack the proper facilities and caregivers to provide the needed services. The states need to implement mental health plans, or they will risk overloading hospitals with psychiatric patients.

The problem is not new. It took root with the elimination of long-term psychiatric facilities that began in the 1950s and continued through the 1980s, in the belief that they were inhumane and that patients would do better if reintroduced into their communities with the benefit of new antipsychotic medication. But those community-based programs never materialized. Though deinstitutionalization may have been well intended, it left people with severe mental illness with no place to go. Many ended up homeless, in conflict with law enforcement, and either incarcerated or brought to our emergency departments. One recent study, using data from 2008 to 2014, found that the proportion of emergency department visits for mental health disorders increased from 8.3 percent to 10.2 percent. And that was before the pandemic.

What's the solution? There is no easy answer, but Lisa McCanna, Atrium Health's senior vice president of behavioral health points to three immediate needs: 1. Community resources, including social support, adequate housing, and access to healthcare to prevent people with mental illness from experiencing a crisis; 2. Individual states' legislatures agreeing to provide adequate funding for mental health care through Medicaid expansion; and 3. Training the providers of tomorrow, as we face a shortage of psychiatrists and other behavioral health practitioners reaching retirement age.

Meanwhile, there are bright spots in the dark clouds of this public health crisis. For one, surveys suggest that the stigma of mental illness is waning. Seventy-six percent of Americans now consider mental health to be as important as physical health. Also, some primary care providers are having behavioral health specialists work right in their offices. For many years, Advocate Health has not only colocated behavioral health providers in the same facility in certain metro Chicago physicians' offices, to remove barriers to care, but it has also integrated behavioral health into the care of patients who need specialized attention. Embedded behavioral health clinicians have access to the same electronic health record (EHR) and regularly consult with primary care physicians about treatments and medications. The result is a more proactive approach for identifying patients with behavioral health conditions and for providing care and treatment earlier. Even when psychiatrists cannot be embedded in the PCP setting, virtual healthcare is helping us reach patients where they are. McCanna's team has created a virtual protocol for providing care while the patient is still in the doctor's office.

"When someone is in the depth of depression, you can't hand them a card and say, 'Call this number,'" she says. "The patient doesn't have the motivation to do that, so we screen the patient while we still have them in the primary care office." The physician will connect the patient via computer monitor to one of our therapists, who conducts an in-depth virtual screening. The therapist then consults with a psychiatrist, who gives care recommendations, including medication that the primary care provider can prescribe, and connects the patient to the appropriate outpatient service. "If we find that the patient is in crisis, we can coordinate admission to inpatient care through the virtual system as well," says McCanna. It happens immediately, while the patient is still in the doctor's office. "We've seen great results," says McCanna. "Not only are we getting people connected to the right level of care, but we've also seen significant improvements in their physical health."

We have these connections between primary care and behavioral health all over our organization's geographic footprint, and the model continues to bear fruit, making it clear that reducing the friction for patients in need of mental health care is transformative. In fact, across the six states where Advocate Health operates, we have four freestanding inpatient psychiatric facilities, in addition to fifteen inpatient psychiatric units in our acute care facilities. We have also integrated behavioral healthcare into seventy-seven of our primary care practices, and we provide school-based behavioral healthcare to K–12 students. As of the fall of 2023, we will be in 114 schools.

One shining example is in Wisconsin, where we are leading the way in innovating new models of care delivery for behavioral health. Advocate Aurora Health, along with three other health systems and Milwaukee County, opened an emergency mental health department in Milwaukee in 2022, as a community resource for patients experiencing a mental health crisis.

PRESCRIPTION SEVEN

Make firearm safety and violence prevention a public health imperative

A team of doctors and nurses rushed into the operating room on the eleventh floor of Atrium Health Carolinas Medical Center, the region's only level one trauma center. Before them lay a thirteen-year-old victim of gunshot wounds. Trauma surgeons worked feverishly to stabilize the boy. He was lucky. A fourteen-year-old victim of the same shooting had died at the scene.

The drama that played out that April evening in Charlotte in 2022 is all too common. In 2021, our health system treated 703 patients with injuries from gun violence, up from 457 in 2017. Of the patients treated in 2021, 9 percent were between ages fifteen and nineteen, while 5 percent were under fifteen.

Emergency department doctors, trauma surgeons, and nurses across our large health system are tired of it. They are tired of the seemingly endless stream of ambulances delivering victims of firearm violence, many of those victims as young as their own children. They are exhausted from the emotional anguish of having to tell another mother their child has perished.

Multiply that scenario at Carolinas Medical Center by the thousands of emergency departments in hospitals across the country. More than 45,200 firearm-related deaths occur in the United States every year, mostly in urban settings.[4] Firearms kill more children and adolescents than motor vehicle accidents. Many die in their own homes. We know that locking up guns and ammunition reduces the risk of self-inflicted and unintentional injury to kids by 85 percent, and yet an estimated 4.6 million kids live in homes with unlocked, loaded guns.[5]

"We've always had more gunshot victims in the eighteen- to twenty-nine age group, but the last couple of years, since COVID, we've seen more teens, thirteen-year-olds, and younger," said trauma surgeon David Jacobs, MD, the medical director of Atrium Health's hospital-based violence intervention program. "And we've seen a change in the type of weapons being used, more semiautomatic weapons and guns with a more devastating impact."

There is no simple answer to preventing another fourteen-year-old from being killed, another Uvalde or Sandy Hook shooting, or another teenager from taking his life, but we can make firearm injury and violence prevention a public health priority. It's about preventing firearm injury and death by demanding a public health approach. After all, gun violence is a public health epidemic.

"Violence is a disease," says Dr. Jacobs. "The way to address this issue is to look at it as a disease that has specific causes and specific treatment strategies. When you look at it as a disease and think about who should be addressing disease in the community, it ought to be the health departments and your health institutions."

We've done it before. Scientific research and health data collection have helped us develop commonsense interventions to eradicate communicable diseases, reduce smoking-related deaths, lower the incidence of heart disease, and make people aware of how a healthy lifestyle impacts cancer risk. Public health initiatives successfully drove seat belt compliance, which cut the annual vehicle fatality rate in half.

There's a significant economic incentive for addressing the disease of violence as a public health imperative, too. Atrium Health's Carolinas Medical Center is the "safety net" hospital in Charlotte, so gunshot victims are often brought to us. Many of these patients are uninsured or underinsured, so our healthcare system bears the cost of taking care of this patient population. So, like many health issues, it's more cost effective to prevent the disease than to be responsible for paying for it once the disease is full-blown.

Several years ago, Dr. Jacobs gave a presentation to me on violence in the Charlotte region, how it impacted Atrium Health, and ways that our hospital system could help. We invited some representatives from the Charlotte City Council and Mecklenburg County to that meeting.

Jacobs told us about the success of violence prevention programs that other hospital systems in Philadelphia, Boston, and elsewhere had adopted. He explained that a hospital-based violence intervention program is based on the notion that if someone is injured seriously enough to wind up at a hospital, it may be a teachable moment, an opportunity for self-reflection, to ask, "How did I end up here, and do I need to think about making some changes in my life?" While we have a captive audience in the hospital, we should do an assessment of their social needs, ask how they came to be a victim of violence, and see if we can develop a prescription that can reduce their chances of becoming victims of violence again. Jacobs said a victim of violence who is injured seriously enough to need a hospital has a 20 to 40 percent chance of coming back as a victim of violence again or becoming a perpetrator of violence. And that multiplies the financial burden of treating the injured. People who sustain violent injuries had median hospital charges of $23,712. Over the course of a seven-year study of treatment for gun violence conducted by Atrium Health, overall hospital charges topped $53 million. Nearly half of patients treated had no health insurance; another 37 percent were covered by Medicare or Medicaid.

After Dr. Jacobs's presentation, Charlotte City Council members recognized the opportunity to interrupt that cycle of violence. The council ultimately agreed to fund a hospital-based violence intervention program at Carolinas Medical Center. We now have two full-time violence interventionalists who see patients who show up at Carolinas Medical Center with gunshots, stab wounds, or other results of violence and will talk to the family, find out the social support structure, and do a 360-degree evaluation of the victim's social needs. They find out if they need alcohol or drug rehab, help getting out of a gang, safe housing, GED training, mental health support, and so on. We know that all of those needs are the fundamental causes of violence, so if we can address those issues and establish a relationship while the patient is present, then we may be able to begin to treat that disease of violence. Our counselors then follow patients after they're discharged from the hospital for six months to a year, until they feel comfortable that the patient's social needs have been met and they are at no higher risk for violence.

We need everyone at the table
While hospital-based violence prevention is a huge step forward, a public health approach for preventing firearm injury and violence is long overdue. We must take a population-level approach that addresses firearm access and all the influences that contribute to gun violence. And let me be clear: This isn't about the Second Amendment or a politicized conversation about firearms. It's about conducting research and collaborating.

Researchers and policymakers must have reliable data to understand the complexity of gun violence and potential prevention strategies. That work is finally starting to be done. In 2019, Congress reached a deal to fund gun violence prevention research through a $25 million allocation to the CDC and the National Institutes of Health (NIH).

But more must be done. As I've mentioned before, research estimates that 60 percent of premature deaths in the United States are caused by nonmedical, socioeconomic factors—the social determinants of health. These are racial disparities, inequality, lack of safe housing, poverty, and inadequate education. All these root causes of health inequities are risk factors for firearm injury.

Gun violence and suicide by firearm disproportionately impact economically disadvantaged groups. Substandard education, poor job prospects, food and housing instability, and inadequate access to healthcare compromise social cohesion and community safety, which increases the risk for firearm violence. So, a significant part of the solution must include eliminating the vast disparities in the social determinants of health.

It's not impossible to make violence statistics go down. Several cities, including Oakland, California, and Boston, Massachusetts, have launched large, multifaceted community violence intervention programs involving partnerships between community organizations, local businesses, social service providers, and law enforcement. A similar violence prevention program launched in Mecklenburg County within the last couple of years. These campaigns identified neighborhoods and individuals at high risk for engaging in violence and provided mentoring, counseling, education, and direct assistance. They focused on reducing gang violence, improving responses to family- and gender-based violence, and community healing and restoration projects. And they've been successful in reducing gun violence, by bringing everyone to the table. They have engaged stakeholders in the communities, as well as law enforcement, faith communities, the corporate business community, county and local governments, and those who want to protect gun-owners' rights.

"We tend to talk about gun violence as if it is all one issue, and sometimes that's colored by a political narrative," says Layla Soliman, MD, a forensic psychologist at Atrium Health Behavioral Health in Charlotte. "It's not about politics. It's about meeting patients where they are."

One way we're meeting patients where they are is with a powerful model around supporting survivors of violence that Advocate Aurora Health deployed in Chicago. The Advocate Trauma Recovery Center provides a holistic approach to healing, serving survivors of intentional violence and family members of homicide victims across eight counties in the Chicagoland area. A multidisciplinary team of psychologists, social workers, psychiatrists, outreach workers, and others provide in-person, community-based, and virtual programs at no cost to clients, to meet a wide range of needs. We know that the circumstances that lead to violence are complex, as are their aftereffects, so while we may first cross paths with our clients in a healthcare setting, the Center's care doesn't end when physical wounds heal.

We Must Protect Our Healthcare Heroes from Violence

Every day in our emergency departments, we see the bloody result of the violence taking place in our streets, homes, businesses, and schools. But the violence doesn't stop at our doors. A survey from the American College of Emergency Physicians found that eight in ten emergency physicians believe the rate of violence in emergency departments has increased, and 45 percent said it had increased greatly over the past five years, exacerbated by the pandemic. Nurses, doctors, and other teammates who do heroic work for the public at their most vulnerable times must be protected. Congress should make violent acts against medical professionals a federal offense, just as it is for flight attendants.

PRESCRIPTION 8

Achieve carbon neutrality and protect our planet for future generations
Primum non nocere; "First, do no harm."

Attributed to the ancient Greek physician Hippocrates, it is the ethical cornerstone of the medical profession. Hospitals and their clinicians live by this principle every day, and yet we must remember that the promise extends beyond our walls.

In our work as healers, we are also harming our planet and its inhabitants through the production of pollutants. It has been estimated that healthcare generates nearly 600 million metric tons of carbon dioxide—equivalent to 10 percent of the nation's greenhouse gases—and thousands of tons of medical waste, some of it highly toxic. Hospitals are often the largest consumers of water in a community.

We know that the health of our environment is inextricably connected to human health. The World Health Organization has declared climate change the biggest single threat facing humanity. As chairman of the Federal Reserve Bank of Richmond, I saw the research the Fed has done on the impact of climate change on our economy, now and into the future. Climate shocks from extreme weather events are likely to continue to fuel population migration and lead to widespread loss of housing and jobs. There is an increasingly clear consensus on the cataclysmic damage being done and the consequences of inaction.

Being committed to equity also compels us to act on climate change. As we see more severe weather events, droughts, floods, heat waves, hurricanes, and more, it is clear that those who are already the most marginalized and often living paycheck to paycheck are hit hardest. These communities bear the brunt of asthma and lung cancer, which is exacerbated by air pollution, including mold and toxins that rise after events like major hurricanes. These populations are at far greater risk of dying from extreme climate-related causes, too, or losing their homes because of skyrocketing prices for fuel or air conditioning. On everything from childhood asthma to diabetes, climate change is a key and growing amplifier.

U.S. healthcare must be part of the cure. I have two sons, ages twenty-eight and twenty-two, who remind me of that fact every chance they get. They point out that our industry can take greater steps toward reducing our climate impact and that we must do a better job of measuring, reporting, and improving those efforts. In short, we must lead.

We can have a significant impact, starting with simple changes, as we build toward more ambitious work. Not long ago, a study by researchers in Sweden broke down the moving parts of the average hospital and identified each area's contribution to global warming. They found that 35 percent of environmental impact comes from heating and electricity alone. The next-closest contributors are catering, building infrastructure, and pharmaceuticals. The study is useful because it pinpoints areas where all hospitals and healthcare entities can make a significant environmental impact just by making small changes. For example, in our operating rooms, physician-led teams are eliminating desflurane and reducing nitrous oxide. These two anesthetic gases have the greatest impact on global warming impact and alone account for 1–2 percent of our total emissions.

We have brought together educators from across our system, to integrate climate health and sustainability curriculum into our training of medical students, residents, and senior physicians. We created an Environmental Action Council that leads strategic and operational changes across our enterprise and "green teams" charged with developing innovative solutions for reducing our carbon footprint. Each quarter, our teams host "green tea chats" with experts and speakers from the community, who update us on sustainability efforts and ideas.

Sixty-four percent of U.S. healthcare sector carbon emissions come from the supply chain—from production, transport, use, and disposal of materials that health facilities consume—according to the Healthcare Climate Council. And that doesn't take into consideration employee or patient transportation. Atrium Health was one of the first healthcare systems to sign the White House Healthcare Sector Pledge. In addition to pledging to reduce carbon emissions 50 percent by 2030, we promised to achieve net-zero emissions by 2050. As Advocate Health, we have pledged to achieve carbon neutrality by 2030, and we are striving for net-zero carbon by 2035.

A big part of our success hinges upon investing in heating fuel and electricity conservation measures across our system, transitioning to renewable energy, exploring the electrification of fleet vehicles, and developing a comprehensive commuting program, to encourage the use of public transportation by teammates and minimizing the number of single-occupancy vehicles. We're also committed to protecting our patients and teammates by reducing the use of hazardous chemicals and purchasing safer products, including medical devices, lab chemicals, cleaners, disinfectants, flame retardants, and building materials, such as carpeting, flooring, and furniture. And we are always exploring technical advances to reduce the environmental impact of necessary chemicals and gases used in our work. Since 2017, Advocate Aurora Health physician-led teams have used innovative systems to reduce emissions from volatile anesthetic gasses by 55 percent, saving more than $1 million and avoiding the automobile emissions equivalent of 15,300,000 miles of driving.

There are many solutions on the table. None of them are easy, but all are worth our attention:

- Adopt a national environmental sustainability policy for health systems, to establish a standard of best practices and a system of accountability. Each healthcare organization should create a statement of sustainability goals, along with the reasons and motivations for making change, while ensuring that every teammate understands his or her share of responsibility.

- Make sustainability efforts part of the job. Significant improvements can be made simply through education. For example, regulations require healthcare facilities to use red biohazard bags to segregate medical waste from regular garbage. But teammates sometimes make the mistake of placing uncontaminated garbage in red bags. That practice increases the amount of medical waste that needs to be sterilized or incinerated.

- Put resources toward centralizing sustainability programs through establishing leadership teams in specialized areas (energy, purchasing, supply chain, waste, water, etc.). Give them the authority to make high-level decisions that move the ball down the field. And make them accountable. For example, the products and devices we buy—from flame-retardant mattresses to LCD displays and fluorescent lamps—contain hazardous materials and chemicals. Purchasing teams should prioritize suppliers who are committed to lowering the life cycle carbon intensity of their products while offering recycling programs. Health systems should use their purchasing leverage to redefine the medical device market and encourage vendors to make environmental and energy-saving improvements to their products and services.

- Seek funding for sustainability projects by pursuing grants, rebates, donations, power purchase agreements, and low-interest loans.
- Measure and benchmark current energy consumption to establish a baseline for tracking progress. You can't tell where you're going unless you know where you've been. We can improve sustainability efforts and save money by reengineering our heating and cooling plants and updating lighting systems. Let's waste less water by replacing faucets, showers, and toilets with low-flow fixtures.

A health quality leader said to me last year that our environmental impact is a patient safety, quality, and value issue. The framing is simple. He said, "Use less and green the rest." Many of the things we can do today are simple and inexpensive, and they can save us money as well as lessen our impact on the environment. And technical breakthroughs in the decades to come will no doubt supply us with innovations that will help healthcare providers become better providers to the health of our planet.

What Lies Ahead

The potential solutions outlined in this chapter are complex and extremely challenging, and many are controversial. But as Dr. Martin Luther King Jr. once said, "The measure of a person is not where they stand in moments of comfort and convenience, but in moments of challenge and controversy."[6]

The question for all of us is how will our nation stand in this moment of challenge? Clearly, the many crises in healthcare require us to show courage to think differently and act boldly. We can do it. We must do it, to be able to continue to care for our communities, our neighbors, our friends, and our family members.

When I think about what this moment requires of us, I also think about what healthcare could look like in our country, if our smartest thinkers and most tenacious problem-solvers across government, healthcare, and the private sector worked relentlessly to achieve something audacious and transformational.

I shared earlier in this book a story about my Aunt Carmen, whose vibrant life was cut short by a tragic medication error in a hospital in Spain. I've spent my career working to make sure no other family experiences the kind of loss my family did, and it's a reminder of why all of us across the healthcare field do what we do.

But it can't just be about preventing error. My vision for healthcare in America is about something far greater than that. My vision is of a world I want my sons—and all their peers—to inherit, knowing we pushed beyond the boundaries before us to chart a different path.

In closing, let me share what that vision could look like. Meet Maria.

A routine eye exam was the first clue that Maria Morales had a serious health problem. Her ophthalmologist detected the early stages of diabetic retinopathy, a condition that occurs when too much sugar in the bloodstream leads to blockages in the tiny blood vessels in the retina. Her optometrist made an appointment for her with a retina specialist, who prescribed medication and recommended Maria see an endocrinologist, to manage what she suspected was diabetes.

Blood tests, including one called a hemoglobin A1C test, which measures average blood sugar level for the past two to three months, confirmed that Maria had type 2 diabetes.

"I've struggled with my weight since my mid-thirties," said the fifty-three-year-old, "but except for my asthma and some anxiety, I've always been healthy. I rarely have to see a doctor, so I was shocked about diabetes."

Fortunately, Maria has had health insurance since 2016. After going decades without it (she wasn't eligible through her employer's plan because of her part-time status), Maria bought coverage through the health insurance marketplace created by the Affordable Care Act. Before she had insurance, she probably would have declined the advice to see a retina specialist, due to the cost.

Maria's endocrinologist put her on the drug metformin and prescribed a continuous glucose monitor, a CGM for short, to keep track of her blood sugar levels. A CGM is a device a little bigger than a quarter that attaches to the back of the arm and inserts a tiny filament under the skin, where it measures interstitial glucose in the fluid between the cells. It replaces the finger-stick blood test for monitoring blood sugar levels. Applying the CGM doesn't hurt at all, and the device is much easier to use than the finger-stick method; it automatically "talks" to the user's smartphone, tracking blood sugar every five minutes. If Maria's blood glucose rises or drops out of the normal zone, her smartphone chirps to alert her. Maria's smartphone then sends a message to her daughter Gianna's phone, so she can monitor her mom's health as well. Even Maria's endocrinologist, retina specialist, and primary care physician receive the data, so every physician involved in Maria's care is aware of how her medication and the lifestyle changes she's been advised to make are managing her blood sugar.

"I've always loved cookies and cakes," says Maria. "I used to drink a lot of soda and sweet tea. No more, not since I saw what it did to my sugar, the spike up, and the big dip. No wonder I felt so tired all the time."

The exercise physiologist (EP) in Maria's endocrinologist's office gave her a simple exercise routine—walking every day and resistance training twice a week using elastic exercise bands and body weight calisthenics, like squats and lunges, to strengthen her muscles. "Insulin pushes blood sugar into your muscles, so the more muscle you have, the less you have floating in your bloodstream," he explained. The EP also had a degree in nutrition, so he gave Maria and her daughter a meal plan that emphasized lean proteins, healthy fats, and more vegetables, instead of the high-carbohydrate meals Maria was used to. He even gave her healthy recipes that made over some of her favorite Puerto Rican meals, like rice and beans, empanadas, and pasteles.

Within two weeks, Maria has her routine down. She starts her day with Greek yogurt and some whole-grain toast with her coffee, as she checks the weather and the news before work. Her phone alerts her that the pollen count will be high today, so she takes an extra puff from her inhaler. Her asthma is much easier to control, now that her new inhaler talks to her smartphone.

She also checks her blood sugar on her phone after breakfast. Good. It's in range despite the toast she ate. Two hours later, at work, however, her phone chirps, indicating low blood sugar. It makes sense; she feels a little shaky—and hungry. A few minutes later, Gianna (her family care partner) texts her: "Got a notice from the CGM that your sugar is low. Are you having something to eat?"

Within fifteen minutes, Maria receives a phone call—it's an advanced clinical practice nurse (ACP) from her endocrinologist's office, who has received the same alert, to do a quick virtual visit. The ACP pulls up Maria's e-record and suggests what she should eat to bring her blood glucose back into the healthy range.

After they leave the call, the ACP sends Maria a text with links to a nearby urgent care center, with wait times, and explains how to book an online reservation—just in case her blood sugar remains too low—and asks if she needs transportation.

Thirty minutes later, Maria's blood sugar is back in the healthy range and Gianna receives an "all is well" text. Relieved, she calls her mom.

Maria, with the support of her clinical team and Gianna, is on track to manage her diabetes and stick with the new habits she's adopted to stay healthy. She also makes a point to go in to see her primary care doctor every year, for a regular checkup, and builds a relationship of trust with the physician, Dr. Carolina Hernandez, a young Latina doctor who was drawn to the field of medicine as a way of giving back to her community and whose low-interest medical school loans made it possible for her to pass up a more lucrative job in specialized medicine to provide primary care to the primarily Latino neighborhood she grew up in.

Months after her initial diagnosis of diabetic retinopathy, Maria is still managing her condition well and staying on top of her routine, with the help of alerts and texts from her care team and daughter. But the anxiety she's struggled with off and on throughout her life has flared up, and in Maria's regular checkup, Dr. Hernandez can tell she may need some extra support when it comes to mental health. Without Maria even having to leave the office or make a call to follow up on a referral, Dr. Hernandez is able to get a therapist who is on-site to meet with Maria and set her up with some counseling appointments and a few breathing and somatic exercises, to counter the bouts of anxiety when they crop up.

Not only is Maria getting the care she needs—for her mental and physical health—bills are affordable, and she understands what she's being charged for and why. This is a huge relief, after years of struggling to understand what she was going to owe every time she went to the doctor. And when she needs to take a new medication for her asthma, her insurance immediately covers the medication recommended by her doctor, rather than making her take another drug first that might or might not actually help . . . and the medication is within her budget.

Years later, Maria has a bad fall in her kitchen, and an ambulance arrives to take her to the emergency room at the nearest hospital. While Maria doesn't even realize it, the ambulance is an entirely electric vehicle, part of the health system's commitment to curbing carbon emissions and addressing climate change and pollution that disproportionately affects lower-income communities and people of color like Maria. As it turns out, those efforts will help hundreds of children, including Gianna's sons and daughter and Maria's grandchildren, from developing asthma the way Maria did when she was younger.

Healthcare can and should be more like this, from the one-on-one interactions between a patient and the medical assistant checking their vital signs, to the insurance company paying for the medication they need, to the health system doing everything it can to protect the climate for future generations.

The bottom line is that I want to be able to look my boys in the eyes and tell them that I did everything I could to help write that next chapter of health in the broadest sense of the word, health FOR ALL who live in this incredible nation, and that I was joined by hundreds of thousands of others who were unfailingly committed to building a better, brighter future. My hope is that this book shone a light on the incredible heroism of the healthcare heroes on the front lines during the pandemic and in the corners of every community where disparities have existed for far too long. And I hope that the lessons learned, steps taken, and ideas offered here can help all of us work together to make healthcare much better for everyday folks, "the butcher, the banker, the drummer...", as Sly and the Family Stone sang in *Everyday People*. The American people, "from the mountains, to the prairies, to the oceans white with foam," are counting on us to do just that—and deserve no less than health, hope, and healing—*FOR ALL*.

###

Afterword

Friend. Colleague. Partner. These are just a few words that I have had the pleasure of calling Gene throughout our time together in healthcare. And after reading this book, I can now think of a few more: Thought Leader. Innovator. Titan. But, as Gene would say in the humblest of ways, this book is not about him. Rather, it's about an organization—Atrium Health—that has a long and storied history and its vibrant journey adapting in the face of an unprecedented pandemic, building a world-class innovation district, and bringing health, hope, and healing to communities most in need.

Gene and I have known each other for years, as he succeeded me as chair of the American Hospital Association (AHA)—and it was there where I first encountered Gene's sharp policy mind and his steady, visionary leadership. Then as we, Advocate Aurora Health, began to think about the future, my conversations with Gene took on a different tone.

As we broke bread together and became not only colleagues but trusted friends, I learned more about his personal story and his journey as a healthcare leader, a talented musician, a man deeply committed to his family and community. I'm so glad he decided to share some of those pieces of himself with the readers of this book, including our Advocate Health teammates.

As you learned throughout the pages of this book, nonprofit health systems are at a critical precipice in our nation's history. We realized quickly—especially following the passage of the Affordable Care Act—that scale was essential, not only to our success and our ability to serve our communities, but perhaps to our very survival. It's not about scale for the sake of scale; it's that scale done right leads to better outcomes, more opportunity to create jobs and serve our community, and greater access to care for more patients.

That's why I shepherded the organization I was leading, Advocate Health Care in Illinois, through a merger with Aurora Health Care in Wisconsin, back in 2017, creating Advocate Aurora Health. As you read about in chapter 10, at the same time, Gene was doing similar kind of work to grow Atrium Health—bringing Navicent Health, Floyd Health, and Wake Forest Baptist Health into the Atrium Health fold and transforming what had been Carolinas HealthCare System into a regional powerhouse in the Southeast.

And in that same chapter, you read the story of how Gene and I dove into our biggest challenge and greatest opportunity yet—forging a new organization, together.

Gene and I had stayed in touch after I passed the baton to him at the American Hospital Association, and I admired from afar what he was up to in the Southeast, while focused on building Advocate Aurora Health in the Midwest. As I started to think about my plans for retirement and how to best set up my organization for a thriving future in an increasingly challenging environment, Gene was at the top of my list of calls to make.

After months of conversation and deliberation, we announced that Atrium Health and Advocate Aurora Health would come together as one unified organization, called Advocate Health, while maintaining our consumer-facing, care delivery brands in our various markets (Advocate in Illinois, Aurora in Wisconsin, and Atrium in the Southeast).

As I write this, Gene and I have been copiloting this new combined health system for more than half a year, after officially joining forces in early December 2022 as Advocate Health. It has been one of the greatest privileges of my career, and I am confident that Advocate Health is in the best of hands. What Gene built in the Southeast is a tremendous testament to his intellect, his commitment, his leadership, and his perseverance. And I am so proud of what we've built together.

Gene's heart for community and equity, as well as his drive toward innovative and transformational change, will serve Advocate

Health—and the millions of patients we are privileged to serve—well for years to come. I'm proud to call him a friend and colleague and proud he has put this book into the world. What a gift for readers to get to know him and his journey and to learn from his incredible insights about how the nonprofit healthcare sector, and our organization in particular, can catapult into a successful, bright future.

—Jim Skogsbergh
Chief Executive Officer, Advocate Health
July 2023

Endnotes

Author's Note: "I'm Hungry"

1   "Overcoming Obstacles to Health: Report From the Robert Wood Johnson Foundation to the Commission to Build a Healthier America"; http://www.com-missiononhealth.org/PDF/ObstaclesToHealth-Report.pdf

2   American Medical Association, "Inequity's Toll for Black Americans: 74,000 more deaths a year." https://www.ama-assn.org/delivering-care/health-equity /inequity-s-toll-black-americans-74000-more-deaths-year.

3   Dr. Martin Luther King, Jr., "Beyond Vietnam: A Time to Break Silence." (Speech delivered at Riverside Church, New York, NY, April 4, 1967.

4   Institute of Medicine (US) Committee on Understanding and Eliminating Racial and Ethnic Disparities in Health Care, "Unequal Treatment: Confronting Racial and Ethnic Disparities in Health Care," https://pubmed.ncbi.nlm.nih .gov/25032386/.

Chapter 1. "This Is for Real"

1   Shih-Hsiung Chou, et al. "Factors Associated with Rising Risk for Care Escalation Among Patients with COVID-19 Receiving Home-Based Hospital Care." Letter, *Annals of Internal Medicine*, August 2021, acpjournals.org/doi/10.7326/ M21–0409.]

Chapter 2. Vaccines and New Hope

1   CBS, *Face the Nation*, July 26, 2020, https://www.youtube.com/watch?v=IRkiZHSmvMc

2   PBS News, "North Carolina Governor Cooper: 'Unvaccinated people are driving this resurgence,'" September 21, 2021.

Chapter 4. Improvisation: Leading through Crisis

1   *Then Came the Fire: Personal Accounts from the Pentagon, 11 September 2001*, Ed. Stephen J. Lofgren, Center of Military History, United States Army, Washington, D.C., 2011.

Chapter 5. History Has Its Eyes on Us

1   Tom's prophecy became real in 2021 when I was named number 4 on *Modern Healthcare's* list of 100 Most Influential People in Healthcare.
2   Latoya Hill and Samantha Artiga, "COVID-19 Cases and Deaths by Race/Ethnicity: Current Data and Changes over Time." KFF, August 22, 2022, https://www.kff.org/racial-equity-and-health-policy/issue-brief/covid-19-cases-and-deaths-by-race-ethnicity-current-data-and-changes-over-time/.
3   Harriet Washington, *Medical Apartheid: The Dark History of Medical Experimentation on Black Americans from Colonial Times to the Present*, (Anchor Books, New York, NY, 2008), 620–21.
4   NPR, "Medical Apartheid Tracks History of Abuses," January 29, 2007.
5   Greg Johnson, PennToday.com, "The Life and Times of W.E.B. Du Bois at Penn," February 21, 2019, https://penntoday.upenn.edu/news/times-and-life-web-du-bois-penn.
6   W.E.B. Du Bois, *The Philadelphia Negro: A Social Study*, University of Pennsylvania Press, 1899.
7   Michael Blanding, *Harvard Public Health*, "Revisiting the 'Unequal Treatment' report, 20 years later," October 3, 2022, https://harvardpublichealth.org/alumni-post/revisiting-the-unequal-treatment-report-20-years-later/.
8   César Caraballo et al, "Excess Mortality and Years of Potential Life Lost Among the Black Population in the US, 1999–2020," *JAMA*, May 16, 2023, https://pubmed.ncbi.nlm.nih.gov/37191702/.
9   American Academy of Family Physicians, "Poverty and Health–The Family Medicine Perspective (Position Paper)," https://www.aafp.org/about/policies/all/poverty-health.html.
10 Raj Chetty et al, "The Association Between Income and Life Expectancy in the United States, 2001–2014," *Journal of the American Medical Association*, April 26, 2016, https://pubmed.ncbi.nlm.nih.gov/27063997/.
11 Sofia Carratala and Connor Maxwell, "Health Disparities by Race and Ethnicity," Center for American Progress, May 7, 2020, https://www.americanprogress.org/article/health-disparities-race-ethnicity/.
12 *Modern Healthcare*, June 11, 2020: https://www.modernhealthcare.com/providers/how-healthcare-can-heal-racism.
13 Lyndon B. Johnson, Radio and Television Remarks Upon Signing the Civil Rights Bill, The American Presidency Project, July 2, 1964, https://www.presidency.ucsb.edu/node/239092
14 Marcella Aslan, Owen Garrick, and Grant Graziani, "Does Diversity Matter for Health? Experimental Evidence from Oakland," Stanford Institute for Economic Policy Research, 2018, https://siepr.stanford.edu/publications/working-paper/does-diversity-matter-health-experimental-evidence-oakland

Chapter 6. Not Enuff Joy

1   Merriam-Webster, "woke," accessed June 28, 2023, https://www.merriam-webster.com/dictionary/woke.
2   Nicholas Janni, *Leader as Healer,* LID Publishing, London, UK, 2022.

3   Alexandra Alter, "Amanda Gorman Captures the Moment, in Verse," *New York Times*, January 19, 2021, https://www.nytimes.com/2021/01/19/books/amanda-gorman-inauguration-hill-we-climb.html

Chapter 7. Meeting the Workforce Challenge: How to Grow the Next Generation of Healthcare Professionals

1   "The Complexities of Physician Supply and Demand: Projections from 2019 to 2034," AAMC; https://www.aamc.org/media/54681/download?attachment.
2   U.S. Bureau of Labor Statistics Occupational Outlook Handbook Registered Nurses, https://www.bls.gov/ooh/healthcare/registered-nurses.htm.
3   The 2020 National Nursing Workforce Survey, https://www.journalofnursing regulation.com/article/S2155–8256(21)00027–2/fulltext.
4   U.S. Healthcare Labor Market, Mercer, https://www.mercer.us/content/dam /mercer/assets/content-images/north-america/united-states/us-healthcare-news /us-2021-healthcare-labor-market-whitepaper.pdf.
5   National Academy of Medicine, "Taking Action Against Clinician Burnout: A Systems Approach to Professional Well-Being," October 2019, https://nam.edu /wp-content/uploads/2019/10/CR-report-highlights-brief-final.pdf.
6   "Prevalence of Burnout Among Respiratory Therapists Amid COVID-19 Pandemic," *Respiratory Care Journal*, https://rc.rcjournal.com/content/66/11/1639.
7   Medscape National Physician Burnout & Suicide Report, 2021, https://www .medscape.com/slideshow/2021-lifestyle-burnout-6013456?faf=1.
8   KFF/The Washington Post Frontline Healthcare Workers Survey, April 2021, https://www.kff.org/report-section/kff-the-washington-post-frontline-health -care-workers-survey-toll-of-the-pandemic/.
9   Nursing CE Central 2021 Nurse Burnout Study 2021, https://nursingcecentral .com/nurse-burnout-study-2021/.
10 "Medical Student Education: Debt, Costs, and Loan Repayment Fact Card for the Class of 2021," AAMC, https://store.aamc.org/downloadable/download/sample /sample_id/468/.
11 "The Medical Laboratory Personnel Shortage," ACSP, https://www.ascp.org /content/docs/default-source/policy-statements/ascp-pdft-pp-med-lab-personnel -short.pdf?sfvrsn=2.
12 American Hospital Association, "#123forEquity Campaign to Eliminate Health Care Disparities," accessed May 12, 2023, https://ifdhe.aha.org/123forequity.
13 Jacqueline Howard, "Only 5.7% of US doctors are Black, and experts warn the shortage harms public health," CNN, February 21, 2023, https://www.cnn .com/2023/02/21/health/black-doctors-shortage-us/index.html.

Chapter 8. The Pearl: Ground Zero for Education, Innovation, and Healing

1   Vince Graham, "Urban Renewal . . . Means Negro Removal. ~ James Baldwin (1963)" YouTube video, accessed March 17, 2023, https://www.youtube.com/ watch?v=T8Abhj17kYU.

2 Drew Boolea, "Report Details Decades Of Systemic Racism In Mecklenburg County," *WCCB*, February 14, 2022, https://www.wccbcharlotte.com/2022/02/14/report-details-decades-of-systemic-racism-in-mecklenburg-county/.

3 Alyssa Wiltse-Ahmad, *National Community Reinvestment Coalition*, "Study: Gentrification and cultural displacement most intense in America's largest cities, and absent from many others," March 18, 2019, https://ncrc.org/study-gentrification-and-cultural-displacement-most-intense-in-americas-largest-cities-and-absent-from-many-others/.

4 Renewing Inequality: Urban Renewal, Family Displacements and Race, 1950–1966, https://dsl.richmond.edu/panorama/renewal/#view=0/0/1&viz=cartogram.

5 Hannah De Los Santos et al, "From Redlining to Gentrification: The Policy of the Past that Affects Health Outcomes Today," *Harvard Medical School Primary Care Review*, May 26, 2021, https://info.primarycare.hms.harvard.edu/review/redlining-gentrification-health-outcomes.

6 Jeremy Markovich, "The Man Who Built Charlotte," *Our State*, Oct 23, 2017, https://www.ourstate.com/hugh-mccoll-charlotte-banking/.

7 *Charlotte News*, June 25, 1936.

8 *Charlotte Evening Chronicle*, September 24, 1891, p. 4.

9 *Journal of the American Medical Association*, March 30, 1929, pp. 1096–98.

Chapter 9. How Healthcare Works in America

1 Healthtracker.org, "How does health spending in the U.S. compare to other countries?" February 9, 2023.

2 Kiku Adatto, "Sound Bite Democracy: Network Evening News Presidential Campaign Coverage, 1968 and 1988," Shorenstein Center Research Paper Series 1990, R-2, Harvard University, Cambridge, MA, June 1990.

3 Kyle Dropp and Brendan Nyhan, "One-Third Don't Know Obamacare and Affordable Care Act Are the Same," *New York Times*, February 7, 2017. https://www.nytimes.com/2017/02/07/upshot/one-third-dont-know-obamacare-and-affordable-care-act-are-the-same.html.

4 Kirzinger et al, "KFF Health Tracking Poll – March 2022: Economic Concerns and Health Policy, The ACA, and Views of Long-term Care Facilities," KFF, March 31, 2022, https://www.kff.org/health-costs/poll-finding/kff-health-tracking-poll-march-2022/.

5 Kevin B. O'Reilly, "1 in 3 doctors has seen prior auth lead to serious adverse event," AMA, March 29, 2023, https://www.ama-assn.org/practice-management/prior-authorization/1-3-doctors-has-seen-prior-auth-lead-serious-adverse-event.

6 Kenneth Kaufman, "Kenneth Kaufman: Why hospitals need scale," American Hospital Association, December 18, 2018, https://www.aha.org/news/insights-and-analysis/2018-12-18-kenneth-kaufman-why-hospitals-need-scale#:~:text=Scale%20will%20help%20ensure%20that,pricing%20is%20of%20minor%20consequence.

Chapter 10. Do More, Be Better, Go Faster

1   Jim Butcher, *Death Masks: The Dresden Files - Book Five* (New York, N.Y., New American Library, 2003).

Chapter 11. Eight Prescriptions for the Future of Healthcare *For All*

1   Centers for Disease Control and Prevention, "Health and Economic Benefits of High Blood Pressure Interventions," December 21, 2022, https://www.cdc.gov /chronicdisease/programs-impact/pop/high-blood-pressure.htm

2   Geneviève Arsenault-Lapierre et al. "Hospital-at-Home Interventions vs In-Hospital Stay for Patients With Chronic Disease Who Present to the Emergency Department: A Systematic Review and Meta-analysis." *JAMA*, network open vol. 4. 6 e2111568, June 1, 2021, https://www.ncbi.nlm.nih.gov/pmc/articles /PMC8188269/#:~:text=This%20systematic%20review%20of%209,had%20 a%20lower%20risk%20for

3   O.J. Wouters et al., "Association of Research and Development Investments with Treatment Costs for New Drugs Approved From 2009 to 2018," *JAMA Net Open*, 2022;5(9):e2218623, doi:10.1001/jamanetworkopen.2022.18623.

4   John Gramlich, "What the data says about gun deaths in the U.S.," Pew Research Center, April 26, 2023, https://www.pewresearch.org/short-reads/2023/04/26 /what-the-data-says-about-gun-deaths-in-the-u-s/

5   M. Miller and D. Azrael, "Firearm Storage in US Households With Children: Findings From the 2021 National Firearm Survey." *JAMA Netw Open,* 2022;5(2):e2148823. doi:10.1001/jamanetworkopen.2021.48823

6   Dr. Martin Luther King, Jr., in a sermon delivered August 1958 at the first National Conference on Christian Education of the United Church of Christ at Purdue University.